A Way of Life in the World

Spiritual Practices for United Methodists

Kenneth H. Carter, Jr.

Abingdon Press
Nashville

A WAY OF LIFE IN THE WORLD:
SPIRITUAL PRACTICES FOR UNITED METHODISTS

Copyright © 2004 by Abingdon Press

This book is printed on acid-free paper.

Library of Congress Cataloging-in-Publication Data

Carter, Kenneth H.
A way of life in the world : spiritual practices for United Methodists
/ Kenneth H. Carter, Jr.
   p. cm.
   ISBN 0-687-02246-0 (adhesive binding : alk. paper)
   1. Spiritual life—United Methodist Church (U.S.) 2. United Methodist Church (U.S.)—Doctrines. I. Title.

BX8349.S68C37 2004
248.4'876—dc22

                    2003024012

(Copyright page continued on page 4.)

04 05 06 07 08 09 10 11 12 13—10 9 8 7 6 5 4 3 2 1

MANUFACTURED IN THE UNITED STATES OF AMERICA

For friends in each congregation
who have shared this way of life with our family

Contents

Acknowledgments

I write to you about a Church, a tradition that has been a means of grace for me. This perspective is neither romantic, naïve, nor, I hope, arrogant. There are many living streams of Christian tradition. By God's providence I have stepped into this one stream, and its waters have cleansed and nourished me. I appreciate the convictions that are at the core, and yet I am also grateful for the amazing diversity that is experienced in congregations across our denomination. Even among the congregations I have served— a four-point charge, a new congregation, three larger congregations—there has been a diversity of belief and practice. And yet each church, and many others with whom I have been privileged to share, has been at its core thoroughly Methodist in its Christian expression.

The origin of this book came to me through participation over a couple of years with a small group of pastors from across the United States. They represented Presbyterian, Baptist, Disciple, Roman Catholic, Episcopal, United Church of Christ, and Lutheran traditions. I was there as a United Methodist. I am grateful to Lillian Daniel, Michael Thurman, Arthur Boers, Ann Svennungsen, Michael Mooty, Mary Graves, Felicia Thomas, Nick Rice, David Musgrave, Jack Wall, and Ted Wardlaw, and our conveners, David Wood (then of the Louisville Institute) and James Lewis (of the Louisville Institute) and Craig Dykstra and Chris Coble of the Lilly Endowment. The experience of spending time in study and fellowship, conversation, and worship with pastors deeply committed to their own traditions led me back to my own with a fresh appreciation.

A part of our time together was spent in reflection on the concept of practices, and for me the Wesleyan tradition seemed a natural fit with this very fruitful development in recent theology. Moreover, I became convinced that the local congregation was the laboratory for understanding practices—the daily lives of members and clergy of congregations who live the Christian life—over a span of time. At a basic level, congregations need resources to sustain their mission over generations, and individuals need corresponding disciplines if their commitments are to endure. The concept of practices and the unique traditions of the Wesleys and their descendants seemed to come together for me, and I have attempted here to share the fruits of this discovery.

I also want to express my gratitude to two groups who have contributed to the ideas in these pages. A yearlong group met to focus on spiritual practices, and another group met for a year at a later time to focus on distinctively Methodist practices. The latter experience was enhanced by a grant from the Valparaiso Institute, for which I am grateful. Both groups met at Mount Tabor United Methodist Church in Winston-Salem, North Carolina, and I am grateful as well to the staff, the leaders, and the members of that congregation, especially Judy Mahathey, who served as administrative coordinator of the grant. I am grateful to my present congregation, Providence United Methodist Church in Charlotte, North Carolina, for their faithfulness to these core practices of our tradition. I also wish at this point to thank three theologians who have been wonderful teachers to me: Robert Cushman, Thomas Langford, and Ralph Wood.

A last impetus for the book came from participation as a pastor-theologian with the Center of Theological Inquiry, Princeton, New Jersey, from 1999 through 2001. The group, convened by John Stapleton, was ecumenical, and my essay, "The Recovery of Human Nature Through Christian Practice: A Pastoral Inquiry into a Methodist Way of Life," a revision of which later appeared in *Quarterly Review*, grew out of this experience and helped shape the form of this book.

It seems clear to me that John and Charles Wesley were shaped most powerfully by their parents, Samuel and Susanna, and especially Susanna! I want to thank my grandparents, Bill and Bernice Ensminger, and my mother, Frieda Moye. They put me in places to meet Christ, and in their lives I saw the gospel. Mostly, the ordinary channels of grace in my own life have been my wife, Pam, and our daughters, Liz and Abby. Over the last twenty years, Pam and I have shared breakfast together in the mornings, walks at night, and everything in between. We have attended concerts to hear Liz play the viola, and volleyball matches to watch Abby compete. These have been some of our practices. Looking back over a significant span of time, I realize that it has become a way of life.

If Liz and Abby continue to search the Scriptures, speak the truth, break the bread, give to the poor, offer their own music, and search for community, that will be grace enough for me. They are a microcosm of my prayer for the whole church: that we will discover (and rediscover) the riches of God's grace through the ordinary experiences of life that are available to us.

Introduction: Spiritual Practices for United Methodists

These are the things you must insist on and teach. . . . Put these things into practice, devote yourself to them, so that all may see your progress.

—1 Timothy 4:11, 15

I contend that all of the ordinances of God are the stated channels of his grace to [men and women]; and that it is our bounden duty to use them all, at all possible opportunities.

—John Wesley

Action follows vision; and vision depends on character—a person thinking, reasoning, believing, feeling, willing, and acting as a whole.

—Craig Dykstra

What Are Practices?

Many of the activities that fill our schedules and call forth our passions are made possible by practices of one sort or another. A girl loves cheerleading; the practices teach her the rhythms of movement and the sounds of words. A young man loves to play the classical guitar; practice teaches him correct body posture, the importance of tuning, the correct positioning of his hands and fingers. Another man is passionate about fly-fishing. Over time he practices the counterclockwise motion of casting, he learns to tie flies, he becomes adept at reading the waters. A woman loves to work with fabric and her eyes are trained to see the colors and her hands become knowledgeable about texture. In time she becomes more comfortable in her creativity, having mastered the basics and now moving on to new and different possibilities.

Many of us find that when we engage in an activity over time, an activity that includes an ongoing experience of practice of some sort, habits are developed. These habits can become second nature to us: the cheers that a young girl learns, the music of the classical guitarist, the fisherman's art, the seamstress and her relation to the fabric. Of course habits are not always positive: we often call negative habits "addictions." Addictions are habits that have destructive consequences in our lives and in the lives of others.

Habits (understood positively) lead to an increase in freedom. Randy L. Maddox has noted that "Wesley's language of holy actions 'flowing' from holy tempers suggests that he appreciated the sense in which habituated affections bring 'freedom' for human actions—the freedom that comes from disciplined practice."[1] This echoes the teaching of Jesus about the freedom that flows from discipleship: "If you continue in my word, you are truly my disciples; and you will know the truth, and the truth will make you free" (John 8:31-32).

Addictions lead to a decrease in freedom. Habits, as they flow out of Christian practices, are life-giving. Addictions, as they result from abuse of body, mind, or spirit, are death-inducing. The psalmist speaks of a practice that is life-giving:

> Happy are those who do not follow the advice of the wicked, or take the path that sinners tread, or sit in the seat of scoffers; but their delight is in the law of the LORD, and on his law they meditate day and night. They are like trees planted by streams of water, which yield fruit in its season, and their leaves do not wither. In all that they do, they prosper. (Psalm 1:1-3)

In the same psalm, the alternative is also described:

> The wicked are not so, but are like chaff that the wind drives away. Therefore the wicked will not stand in the judgment, nor sinners in the congregation of the righteous; for the LORD watches over the way of the righteous, but the way of the wicked will perish. (Psalm 1:4-6)

One of the earliest Christian documents, the *Didache*, begins with these words: "There are two ways, one of life and one of death, and there is a great difference between the two ways" (1.1). Practices lead to habits, and habits, over the long haul, add up to a way of life. One of the important practices for Israel in the period of Exile was the sabbath.[2] The practice of a day of rest can become a habit—life seems unnatural without it, and the long-term experience of sabbath can be life-giving to our bodies, our minds, and our spirits. In the same way that sabbath is a practice that is beneficial for us, it is also a command of God: "Six days you shall do your work, but on the seventh day you shall rest" (Exodus 23:12).

In like manner, the Lord's Supper is also a practice that can become a life-giving habit. John Wesley, in his sermon "On the Duty of Constant Communion" noted that we are to receive the Lord's Supper because it is commanded by God and because it is for our benefit (to receive mercy).

We are shaped as human beings by practices. We are creatures of habit. We often come to these practices in the presence of guides, mentors, companions, and leaders. One image for the process is *apprenticeship*. Greg Jones has likened the story of Noah Adams, who at age fifty-one decided to learn to play the piano, to the process of becoming a disciple. Adams tried various shortcuts before undertaking the discipline required to progress. Jones writes:

> Just as Adams decided to take up the piano as an adult, so many adults these days are deciding to seek out the church. Some have had childhood lessons in being a Christian, but left the church for many years. Many people who are taking up the church have had little if any exposure to the Christian faith. . . . How can they learn to practice Christianity?
>
> One temptation is to look for shortcuts. . . . But shortcuts are not likely to teach us the truth about God and ourselves. There is no substitute for the slow, sometimes painful growth that comes through disciplined habits of practice shaped by the grace of the crucified and risen Christ. One does not become an excellent piano player, painter or a soccer star overnight; neither does one learn to become a Christian overnight. One needs teachers and mentors.[3]

Teachers and mentors in the faith guide us in the sometimes difficult and arduous journey of growth in grace. The moral theologian

NOMINAL 13 CHRISTIAN vs.
PRACTICING CHRISTIAN!

Stanley Hauerwas has likened the Christian life to the process of becoming a bricklayer. The church's problem, he suggests, is that we focus exclusively either on being a caring community or a believing community. But care is often disconnected from discipline, and belief is often perceived in a vacuum, apart from a formative community. He insists:

> To help us get a better picture of what it means for the church to be a disciplined community, we ought to learn how to lay a brick. This discipline will help us think about what it means to be saved, what it means to be a Christian. To learn to lay brick, it is not sufficient for you to be told how to do it, but you must learn a multitude of skills. . . . Moreover, it is not enough to be told how to hold a trowel, how to spread mortar, . . . but in order to lay brick you must hour after hour, day after day, lay brick. . . . All of this indicates that to lay brick you must be initiated into the craft of bricklaying by a master craftsman.[4]

The process of becoming a bricklayer, Hauerwas suggests, is transforming, even converting, "like that of making oneself an apprentice to a master of a craft."[5] Of course, becoming a Christian is an apprenticeship to Jesus and his disciples, a way of life that is learned as we do specific practices. Another image, more explicitly found in Christian tradition, is *imitation*. Paul writes to the church at Philippi, "Brothers and sisters, join in imitating me, and observe those who live according to the example you have in us" (Philippians 3:17).

Imitation is another way that we enter into practices. We are invited into a way of life in the same manner that Jesus called Simon and Andrew (Mark 1:16-20; John 1:40-41). This is the call to discipleship, which is itself a set of practices and habits. Biblical scholars have reflected on the prominence of imitation in Christian history. The call to imitation was widespread in classical education (Aristotle, Plato), and was later present in a number of New Testament passages:

> Remember your leaders, those who spoke the word of God to you; consider the outcome of their way of life, and imitate their faith. (Hebrews 13:7)
> For to this you have been called, because Christ also suffered

14

for you, leaving you an example, so that you should follow in his steps. (1 Peter 2:21)

Christianity is a living faith, practiced over time by disciples (learners). This living tradition has come to us as United Methodists through the practices of John and Charles Wesley, and those who imitated them. Of course, we imitate the Wesleys because we see their lives as imitations of Jesus Christ. In this way each reformation of the church is in some sense a recovery of an aspect of Christian tradition that has been neglected:

- Francis and his compassion for the poor
- Luther and his reliance on grace alone
- Teresa and her grasp of mysticism
- Calvin and his insistence on the sovereignty of God
- Wesley and his focus on scriptural holiness
- Barth and his entrance into the strange new world of the Bible
- King and his vision of the kingdom of God
- Romero and his passion for the oppressed

These reformations, and many others throughout Christian history, are also arguments against the status quo, with the institutionalized forms of church that had become dominant.

FOR REFLECTION: HOW HAS THE INSTITUTIONALIZED FORM OF CHURCH, IN YOUR EXPERIENCE, IGNORED A VITAL DIMENSION OF AUTHENTIC CHRISTIANITY?

Discipleship is not only an apprenticeship and imitation of what a Christian life should look like, but it is also a response to what the Christian life *is not*. In the liturgy of the Baptismal Covenant, a renunciation of sin is placed alongside a profession of faith, "Do you renounce the spiritual forces of wickedness, reject the evil powers of this world, and repent of your sin? . . . Do you accept the freedom and power God gives you to resist evil, injustice, and oppression in whatever forms they present themselves?"[6]

The early church understood discipleship as a form of *spiritual resistance* (James 4:7; 1 Peter 5:9). And as Christians in the twenty-first century we find ourselves, at times, saying yes and at other times saying no![7]

A Practice Is an Extended Argument with the Desire for Immediate Results

In his magisterial work *After Virtue,* Alasdair MacIntyre suggests that a living tradition is "an historically extended, socially embodied argument."[8] As a tradition, Christianity is a set of practices, some of them described later in this book, that form an argument against something. A practice itself, since it requires training, repetition, learning, and a span of time, is an argument against one of our culture's fundamental premises: the desire for immediate results.

The New Testament itself can be understood as an "historically extended, socially embodied argument" against some of the cultural assumptions of both Jewish and Gentile worlds: attitudes about women, customs among economic and social classes, interpretations of the law. We recall the refrain of the teaching of Jesus in the Sermon on the Mount, which is itself a form of spiritual resistance and an argument against the status quo, "You have heard that it was said . . . but I say to you . . . " (Matthew 5:21-22, 27-28, 38-39).

A part of the revolutionary character of the New Testament lies in the extended argument that it offers. And a part of the authenticity of any Christian tradition that wants to recover early Christian practice lies in the rediscovery of this truth: we will be going against some cultural grain when we exercise our faith through these practices. The apostle Paul writes to the Romans, "Don't become so well-adjusted to your culture that you fit into it without even thinking" (Romans 12 *THE MESSAGE*).

A part of the crisis that faces the church is that we are so well adjusted. Do you ever become so well adjusted to your culture that you fit into it without thinking? I wonder about that. I recently read a book of sermons by Peter Storey, who was a Methodist bishop and preacher in South Africa.[9] It is a collection of messages preached in the crucible of a culture of death, the experience of apartheid. Storey helped to integrate the Central Methodist Church in Johannesburg, and in the process his life was threatened a number of times. He notes that although many churches were opposed to apartheid in principle, preachers didn't often speak about it in their sermons. Their sermons, he said, could have been preached anywhere in the world. Most preachers—he does not say this but I would—most preachers had become so well adjusted to their culture that they had fit into it without thinking.

And the next question, logically, is, *Have we done that too?* Alan Greenspan, testifying recently before Congress, noted that our country has been harmed by what he called "infectious greed." Alan Greenspan is not exactly a spokesman for the faith, but I would argue that greed is the most destructive sin facing our nation. I heard someone say recently that the collapses of corporations such as WorldCom and Enron have done more damage to the economy of the United States than the terrorism of September 11. The CEOs of WorldCom and Enron were publicly Christian men—they are leaders in their churches—and yet their decisions and behaviors have affected your life, my life, and the livelihoods of many in our communities. These men lived in a culture that encouraged their greed, supported their greed, and benefited from their greed. And yet you live in this same culture. And so do I.

I don't preach very often about greed, although I believe it is a sin that threatens our way of life, as Christians, as Americans, as families, as individuals. Why don't I preach about greed more often? Could it be that I have become so well adjusted to the culture that I fit into it without thinking?

FOR REFLECTION: TAKE A MOMENT TO DESCRIBE THE CULTURE IN WHICH YOU LIVE. HOW DOES IT RESONATE WITH THE PRACTICE OF CHRISTIAN FAITH? AND HOW IS THIS CULTURE AT ODDS WITH THE FAITH?

Paul's verse about being well adjusted to our culture is about repentance (Romans 12:2). It is also translated in the NRSV as "do not be conformed to this world, but be transformed by the renewing of your minds, so that you may discern what is the will of God." Eugen Rosenstock-Huessy has said that repentance is an "unwillingness to continue."[10] The Hebrew word means to make a 180-degree turn. Now I know that men are not supposed to be able to admit they are lost and ask for directions, but that is precisely the point: "Do not be conformed to this world, but be transformed by the renewing of your minds."

FOR REFLECTION: ASKING FOR DIRECTIONS, IN THE
CHRISTIAN TRADITION, IS THE SEARCH FOR SPIRITUAL
DIRECTION OR SPIRITUAL GUIDANCE. CAN YOU RECALL A TIME
WHEN YOU SOUGHT OUT SPIRITUAL GUIDANCE FROM SOME-
ONE: A PASTOR, A FRIEND, A TEACHER, OR A SMALL GROUP?

What would it mean to experience the renewing of our minds?
Every day we open the newspapers and read about some disastrous economic shift in our society, some scandal in corporate
America or the church, some health problem that is looming for
us just over the horizon. Or we listen to the news and hear of the
abduction of a child or some other act of senseless violence. We
also know enough to know that there are human rights abuses
going on in the Third World, and a famine happening in Africa
that doesn't even reach our radar screens.

The wife of a friend was having surgery. I had visited someone
at the hospital, and it was a hot summer day in North Carolina.
My friend and his wife do not really have a church home. Our
congregation is so wonderful to reach out to our folks in such situations, but I also wondered what it would be like for someone
who was not in a church. So I decided to go by the grocery store,
in a part of town I am not usually in. I got all of the ingredients
for a banana split—the ice cream (although I wondered if it
would melt—it was summer in the Deep South), the nuts, the
whipped cream, the caramel stuff in the bottle. (I got the healthy
version of some of these things.) I was standing in the grocery line
with a couple of really nice people. They looked to be about sixty
years old, this couple. I assumed they were married. They had
that sort of comfort level around each other. They were smiling. I
didn't notice what they were buying, but they looked at what I
had and the woman said, "I think we are coming with you." We
laughed. I didn't explain what I was really up to.

Then their turn came. They had a key chain with the store's
logo on it, which was scanned through the cash register. They had
two items: a small can of the store's generic luncheon meat, and a
bag of frozen tater tots. The total came to $2.95. They had three
dollars, already out. They had bought these two items before, I
figured. And then the woman looked at me on her way out, and
she smiled again, and she said, "You have a blessed day!"

I may not know exactly what it means to have a renewed mind,
but these folks had it. It was an experience of judgment and grace

for me. Judgment that I have so much, and that I live in the midst of a people who have so much. Grace that God gives us what we need, what is sufficient: in that moment maybe a simple meal for a working couple and later maybe a dessert for another couple who have their own challenges and burdens.

The problem of being well adjusted to our culture is that we miss the grace of God, which is the renewing of our minds. To renew our minds is to exchange:

- Hatred for love, which is the legacy of Martin Luther King
- Despair for compassion, which is the legacy of Mother Teresa
- Apathy for discipline, which is the legacy of John Wesley
- Greed for generosity, which is the legacy of that woman in the store for me
- Fear for trust, which is the legacy of Mary
- Retaliation for forgiveness, which is the legacy of Jesus on the cross, "Father, forgive them."

We are pretty well-adjusted people. But God wants to change us. The practices are one of the ways we place ourselves before God, so that our minds might be renewed, so that we might find ourselves closer to the will of God.

FOR REFLECTION: HAVE YOU EVER HAD THE EXPERIENCE OF CHANGING YOUR BEHAVIOR, AND LATER RECOGNIZING A SHIFT IN YOUR THINKING? [11]

This movement in our lives, I will argue, does not happen immediately. It is, in the words of Eugene Peterson, "a long obedience in the same direction." [12] This movement, shaped by practices that form a way of life, is about perseverance. Noah Adams discovered this truth in learning to play the piano. The church is aware of this truth whenever it undertakes the labor of making disciples, which is as difficult and painstaking as laying brick. We continue in the way, even when we are weary, even when we are running against the wind and swimming against the stream. The words of the prophet sustain us in this long obedience:

Have you not known? Have you not heard? The LORD is the everlasting God, the Creator of the ends of the earth. He does

> not faint or grow weary; his understanding is unsearchable. He gives power to the faint, and strengthens the powerless. . . . Those who wait for the LORD shall renew their strength, they shall mount up with wings like eagles, they shall run and not be weary, they shall walk and not faint. (Isaiah 40:28-29, 31)

An argument with someone is a sign that we have not given up! This argument with our culture—of which the apostle and the philosopher speak—is possible insofar as it is *historically extended* and *socially embodied*. And in this way, the history of salvation, beginning with the patriarchs and matriarchs, extending through the prophets and apostles, continuing with the desert fathers and mothers, the saints and reformers and evangelists, portrays the God who has not given up on us, who perseveres, whose historically extended and socially embodied practice is the salvation of humanity through the life, death, and resurrection of Jesus Christ.

What Are Spiritual Practices?

We move now to a discussion of spiritual practices. This is a recognition that some practices are material or physical: engaging in a pursuit that produces financial income, or in exercises that strengthen the body. Without drawing too sharp a distinction between the material and the spiritual, it is clear that material pursuits have, in many instances, a measurable bottom line: net worth in dollars, pounds lost or gained, and so forth. Many of our practices are shaped by the materialism of our culture, and by extension much of our identity is found in materialist practices: making money, enhancing our physical appearance, purchasing forms of transportation, climbing an occupational ladder. The church can reflect the materialism of the culture in its own life and practice. We emphasize numerical gains in membership growth, acquisition of property and real estate, and amounts of money given to annual and capital campaigns and endowments.

We live in a materialistic culture that shapes our ways of thinking and behaving in ways that are so powerful we often do not even think to question them. And yet we also know that materialism, in itself, cannot satisfy us. The teaching of Jesus seems oddly relevant: "Do not work for the food that perishes, but for the food that endures for eternal life" (John 6:27).

Craig Dykstra has observed "the bread that we feed on is the bread of business and busyness and boredom, a bread known both in and out of the church. This bread will not satisfy our deepest hunger."[13] Of course, many of God's children do cry out for bread. The material always has a concrete spiritual meaning. Many Methodists in the country of Bolivia have learned this prayer that echoes the fourth beatitude of Jesus in the Sermon on the Mount (Matthew 5:6):

> Bless our bread.
> For those who hunger, give bread,
> and for those who have bread, give a hunger for justice.
> Bless our bread.

The emptiness of materialism in our North American context has led many to explore the spiritual traditions of New Age movements. *A Course in Miracles*, channeling, and fascination with crystals have appealed to many who are on a spiritual search. The uncritical blending of spirituality and psychotherapy has given individuals a language to describe their challenges, hopes, and hungers. In both respects these movements have entered a vacuum created by the church that has ignored the human desire for community and transcendence.

For a number of years I taught a lay theological education class and used Avery Dulles's *Models of the Church* as a basic text. Dulles describes five basic expressions of the Christian church: herald, mystical communion, servant, sacrament, and institution. After guiding adults through these models, I would often ask a question: Which model best describes the church as you know and experience it? And the almost universal response would be "the church as institution."

More recent spiritual movements have entered into a vacuum created by a church that has become, to a great extent, an institution that has lost touch with its spiritual traditions. This book is a response, in part, to this perception. I am persuaded that there are deep spiritual traditions that lie at the heart of Christianity in general and United Methodism in particular. I would also argue that a great part of John Wesley's intention in eighteenth-century England was the recovery of these spiritual traditions (in particular those of primitive Christianity).[14]

A part of our response to New Age spiritualities and psychotherapeutic faith is a critique of their inadequacies:

- **Absence of incarnation:** the belief that Jesus was divine and came to us in human flesh
- **Tendency toward gnosticism:** a heresy of the early church that divorced spirit and matter, and gave preference to the life of the spirit
- **Denial of community:** the conviction that the individual has all of the resources he or she needs to live a full and complete life apart from others
- **Divorce from tradition:** the sense that we can choose in eclectic ways from those who have gone before us without understanding the historical forces that shaped their traditions
- **Focus on instantaneous spiritual transformation,** to the exclusion of formation over time and cultivation of practices

It is not enough, however, to critique these movements and their inadequacies. We must also pose a constructive alternative to them, one that takes seriously their concern for spiritual growth.

We have also witnessed a renewal of interest in the spiritual practices of other faith traditions: Buddhism, Islam, Judaism. In many respects these faiths are defined by their practices: how a person prays, what a person eats, where a person lives. A few years ago I traveled to Israel with an interfaith, interracial group that crossed ethnic, political, and religious boundaries. One of our visits was to a kibbutz (commune) composed of Christians from Holland. This group had settled in the aftermath of World War II, and their purpose was to make a witness of peace to Jewish people after the Holocaust. They grew flowers and operated a nice and yet simple hotel.

The most remarkable feature about this group of Christians, however, was their spiritual practice. In addition to Christian worship, they also kept a kosher kitchen that allowed them to be more hospitable, and they held to a strict observance of the sabbath. I can still recall a vivid conversation with a Jewish friend as we were leaving the kibbutz: "They practice Shabbat!" he would repeat, scratching his head, "They practice Shabbat!"

In his mind, the practice was at the heart of his faith. And here were outsiders embracing his practice and his faith! The appeal of Buddhism, Islam, and Judaism to many lies in the specific practices found within them: meditation, regularly scheduled prayer and fasting, devotion to Scripture, particular holy days. In this respect they stand as a witness to Christians, and they pose a question to each of us: Can we discover a way of life that is distinctively Christian? My conviction is that the answer to this question requires that we explore our own spiritual practices, ones that are unique to our tradition.

What Are Christian Spiritual Practices?

This explanation of Christian practices, written by two Christians with a deep understanding of the faith as it is lived in congregations, is worthy of our close reading:

> Woven together, Christian practices form a way of life. This way is not shaped primarily by a certain cultural style, class, nationality or age; on the contrary, the way can embrace people in every circumstance, taking different shapes in different times and places. It becomes visible as ordinary people search together for specific ways of taking part in the practice of God, as they faithfully perceive it in the complicated places where they really live. It is like a tree whose branches reach out toward the future, even when the earth is shaking, because it is nourished by living water.[15]

Woven Together

Specific Christian practices are "woven together"; that is, no one Christian practice defines the whole of our faith. For example, Holy Communion cannot be appropriately practiced apart from generosity with the poor. Indeed, this was the critique of the early church's practice by the apostle Paul in 1 Corinthians 10. Scripture cannot be read, and was not intended to be read, in isolation from the Christian community. Christian practices are brought together, like threads of different color in fabric. I learned a chorus as a participant in the "Walk to Emmaus" retreat: "Weave, weave, weave us together, Weave us together, in unity and love."[16]

Dykstra and Bass assume that there are many different Christian practices. A reading of the New Testament bears this out:

- Do this in remembrance of me
- Sing psalms and hymns and spiritual songs
- Devote yourself to the apostles' teaching and the fellowship, to the breaking of bread and the prayers
- Go and make disciples
- Repay no one evil for evil
- Confess your sins to one another
- When you did it unto the least of these, you did it unto me
- Love one another, as I have loved you
- You will be my witnesses
- Pray without ceasing
- Do not neglect to meet together

Each of these practices was a part of the life of the early Christian church. None of them, in and of themselves, fully captures what it means to live as a Christian. Woven together, however, they form a way of life.

Inclusive

This way of life, we have noted, is at times countercultural and at all times transcultural. The Christian way of life cannot be contained within one culture, one racial grouping, one economic class, or one demographic segment of society. We are reminded of this reality each time a child is baptized in The United Methodist Church, as the parents or sponsors renew their own faith:

> Do you confess Jesus Christ as your Savior,
> put your whole trust in his grace,
> and promise to serve him as your Lord,
> in union with the Church which Christ has opened
> to people of all ages, nations, and races? [17]

The history of Christianity can be seen as the reformation of living tradition through changes in specific practices:

- Who can read or interpret Scripture?
- How do we confess our sins?
- Who is welcome in the membership of a church?
- What is authentic worship?
- How are decisions made?
- How are the poor present or absent in the church?

There are often intellectual movements about matters of nature and grace, humanity and divinity, authority and freedom. But these intellectual movements cannot be separated from concrete practices. For example, John Wesley's theology of grace was shaped by the grace he experienced in preaching to the poor.

Ordinary People in Complicated Places

It should also be noted that this way of life is available to ordinary people. At its best, Christianity has never been about our experience of being spectators, watching in the stands as the heroic Christians live out their virtuous or holy callings (and indeed this can happen in Evangelical, Protestant, or Catholic churches!). It is a way of life to which ordinary people are called: Peter, a fisherman; Mary, a teenager; Matthew, a tax collector; Phoebe, a deacon of the church and supporter of the apostle Paul. Each of these ordinary people took part in the practice of God to bring salvation to the world through Jesus Christ.

And each of us practices the faith "in the complicated places where we really live." I am thinking of two faithful Christians who have witnessed to me through their lives. One owned a builder's supply in a small rural community. He had a burden to help those without faith into the church family. His small business was at the crossroads of this small community, and he had an instinctive grasp of how the lives of the people there intersected with each other, in ways that created community and in others that caused division. Another taught elementary school in the inner city for most of her adult life, and each day she was a sacramental presence to the children in her room. She cared about the lives of her children beyond the classroom and long after they had graduated. I was a preacher to each of them. At times I proclaimed the importance of reconciliation to one in the pews who was actually practicing it. At other times I preached about going out into the world with the compassion of Christ, knowing that, in actuality, there were those among us who had been doing that long before I arrived on the scene. These laity were practicing what I was preaching.

People do practice the faith in the complicated places where they live. I also served as pastor to a man named Cecil. He is a quiet and faithful man who displays his faith by the way he lives. One afternoon I was going through the mail in my office when I came across the newsletter of our community's homeless shelter. Cecil had been named "volunteer of the year." This was news to me. Although I frequently saw Cecil around the church, he was not one to draw attention to himself.

Cecil was interviewed in the newsletter about his volunteer activity, and was asked about his motivation for such exemplary service. He said, "I have a brother who is a schizophrenic, and lives in the Pacific Northwest. He also has paranoid delusions, and often feels that people are following him. So he travels from one homeless shelter to another in that part of the country, and sometimes he writes me letters from wherever he is at the time. When I serve the homeless here, I imagine that one of them is my brother."

Of course, one of them is his brother! Matthew 25 is a reminder that Jesus meets us in the complicated places where people really live.

> I was hungry and you gave me food, I was thirsty and you gave me something to drink, I was a stranger and you welcomed me, I was naked and you gave me clothing, I was sick and you took care of me, I was in prison and you visited me. (Matthew 25:35-36)

Like every parable, the parable of the great judgment has an element of surprise. The unlikeliest person rescues the man who was beaten on the road from Jerusalem to Jericho in the parable of the good Samaritan (Luke 10:25-37). A treasure is discovered, hidden in a field (Matthew 13:44). In the parable of the great judgment, we don't really know what we have done, or whom we have done it to! When did we see you hungry? When did we see you a stranger? We can't actually be certain.

The good news or bad news of the parable is that Jesus comes to us in surprising ways, and that his judgment will also take shape in just that way. I have seen this again and again in the church. Folks will go on a mission team, or become involved in tutoring a child in a tough situation, and it is as if something clicks, the "aha!" moment, and they get it. It's like a moment in revival meeting where head and heart come together and it all makes sense. That is you, Jesus, in that child at an inner city school, in that young girl in Guatemala, in that person in our family who needs us the most, in the forgotten homebound member of the church.

It is Jesus—"When you did it unto the least of these, you did it unto me!" It is not always true that people meet Jesus in the church, and then go out into the world to share the message of his love. Sometimes people meet Jesus and fall in love with him in the world, and they come to church to try to figure out what has happened! In this way the church is a community that reflects on the Christian practices that are already happening in the world.

What Are United Methodist Spiritual Practices?

Is there a Christian way of life that is particular to my own tradition, United Methodism?[18] If so, what practices constitute that way of life? Does this way of life shape us in particular ways? Do specific practices form us as people in ways that we can explain theologically?

These are the core questions with which we have to struggle. I serve a congregation that is typical of many healthy mainline congregations in North America: we worship God, we sing, mostly hymns, sometimes a chorus. We offer care to those who are in the midst of crisis. We gather in small groups, sometimes to learn, at other times just to meet each other. We serve those in need in the larger world.

Our church is also typical of many healthy United Methodist congregations in the United States. We have built buildings in recent years and we are paying for them. We have added a worship service and increased the staff. We support the denomination, insofar as we are aware of what is going on with it.

Significant outreach occurs in the community. We embody much of what is best about United Methodism in our institutional life. Which leads me to one of my original questions: Is there a Christian way of life that is distinctively United Methodist? Sometimes folks will ask about our adult Sunday school classes, of which there are several. None is distinctively doctrinal in any way. We are in close proximity to two megachurches: one is Pentecostal, the other is conservative Baptist. Both are strong, healthy congregations, and yet we know we are not like either in most respects. We do not exclude women from clerical leadership. We do not raise our hands in worship. We do not fuse patriotism and faith.

But we cannot be defined by who we are not! Who are we? The answer to this question comes, in part, from reflecting on our origins. Bishop Rueben Job offers this description of the early Methodists:

> Methodist life was marked by a deep and authentic personal piety that led to a broad and uncompromising social involvement. Methodists were known for their prayers and for their commitment to the poor and disenfranchised. This commitment resulted in persistent efforts to build houses of prayer and worship as well as consistent efforts to visit the prisons, build schools and hospitals, and work for laws that moved toward a just and peaceful social order. . . . Because they took their relationship to Jesus Christ with utmost seriousness, their life of prayer and witness was readily identified and often very contagious as many wanted what Methodists appeared to have. Among these Methodist gifts were a certain knowledge of their own salvation, an at-homeness in this world and confidence in the next, a living companionship with a living Christ, and access to the power of God that could and did transform the most broken and hopeless persons into productive, joyful, and faithful disciples. Such was the power of God at work in the way Methodists lived.[19]

I am convinced that people do seek specific ways to practice Christian spirituality. One of the great publishing phenomena of our time has been a book entitled *The Prayer of Jabez*. I first heard about the prayer while visiting family in another state. I had stopped in to see a friend from college who now operates a

Christian bookstore. "You have to read this book! We can't keep it in the store!" he said to me enthusiastically. Written by Bruce Wilkinson, *The Prayer of Jabez* is taken from a little-known passage in the Old Testament. The prayer is simple: "Oh, that You would bless me indeed, and enlarge my territory, and that Your hand would be with me, that You would keep me from evil, that I may not cause pain!" (1 Chronicles 4:10 NKJV).

I returned home, not having read the book (my friend had sold out of them), only to encounter three folks that very week who mentioned the book. I went out and bought a copy. It is a small book, ninety-two pages, and I read it over lunch. It was at times inspiring, and at other times convicting. When I am reading books on the spiritual life I try not to be too analytical or critical. That is very much my nature, and I have learned that it can be a way of avoiding something God might be saying to me. And yet, in reading *The Prayer of Jabez*, and in saying the words prayerfully, I had the sense that something essential was missing.

A few weeks later I was able to begin to make sense out of my emerging response to this book. By now it had sold four million copies. I thought about the good fortune of my college friend, selling all of those thin volumes for ten dollars each. To be honest, there was some envy—why don't my books sell that many copies? I also imagined folks being genuinely helped by the commentary on the prayer. Still, there had to be more. Something was missing.

What was missing became apparent to me as I concluded a year of helping teach *Disciple* Bible Study. At the course's end there is a focus on relationship with God. This relationship is established through covenant, remembered in Holy Communion. Within the service are words similar to this prayer:

> Lord, make me what you will.
> I put myself fully into your hands:
>> put me to doing, put me to suffering,
>> let me be employed for you, or laid aside for you,
>> let me be full, let me be empty,
>> let me have all things, let me have nothing.
> I freely and with a willing heart
>> give it all to your pleasure and disposal.

These words are taken from the Covenant Renewal Service in the Wesleyan tradition.[20] They were published in 1753 by John Wesley, and can be traced to a Puritan text written almost one hundred years earlier. The first covenant service in the Methodist movement was probably celebrated in 1755, according to *The United Methodist Book of Worship*. The service has been a popular one on New Year's Eve, New Year's Day, and on the first Sunday of a New Year.

These words of the covenant prayer have been a part of our devotional life for almost 250 years. With the advent of *Disciple*, they have been introduced to over one million Methodists meeting in small groups. In the voicing of the words at the conclusion of *Disciple*, I realized that our spiritual birthright, as people called Methodist, was not in the prayer of Jabez. Our spiritual heritage is captured in the words of the covenant prayer. They are profoundly biblical and express a radical dependence on God and submission to God's will. They are almost a commentary on a more brief prayer of our Lord: "Not what I want. You, what do you want?" (Matthew 26:39 *THE MESSAGE*). Reading the words of the prayer of Jabez (and Wilkinson's commentary on it) alongside the covenant prayer presents starkly contrasting visions of the Christian life:

- One is about self-fulfillment, the other self-denial
- One is about changing God's mind, the other about submitting to God's purpose
- One is personal, the other is corporate
- One is in harmony with a culture of acquisition and consumption, the other is in conflict with expanding markets and egos

By grace, God welcomes all of our prayers. "We do not know how to pray as we ought," the apostle Paul wrote in Romans 8:26. God takes the inadequacies of all of our prayers—surely my own included—hears our true intentions, and responds. Paradoxically, God did expand the territory of a group of disciples who were shaped by a prayer that asked for nothing other than to be of service to God's will and purpose. My appeal to United Methodists is to recover another prayer that has been practiced for 250 years, a prayer that has been transformative to millions of

believers across the generations, many of whom know the fulfillment of the covenant prayer's concluding petition:

> I am no longer my own, but thine.
> Put me to what thou wilt, rank me with whom thou wilt.
> Put me to doing, put me to suffering.
> Let me be employed by thee or laid aside for thee,
> exalted for thee or brought low for thee.
> Let me be full, let me be empty.
> Let me have all things, let me have nothing.
> I freely and heartily yield all things
> to thy pleasure and disposal.
> And now, O glorious and blessed God,
> Father, Son, and Holy Spirit,
> thou art mine, and I am thine. So be it.
> And the covenant which I have made on earth,
> let it be ratified in heaven. Amen.[21]

PART ONE

The Six Practices

Now pass on this counsel to the Christians there, and you'll be a good servant of Jesus. Stay clear of silly stories that get dressed up as religion. Exercise daily in God—no spiritual flabbiness, please! Workouts in the gymnasium are useful, but a disciplined life in God is far more so, making you fit both today and forever.

—1 Timothy 4 *(THE MESSAGE)*

Come let us use the grace divine,
and all with one accord,
in a perpetual covenant join ourselves
to Christ the Lord;
give up ourselves, thru Jesus' power,
his name to glorify;
and promise, in this sacred hour,
for God to live and die.

—Charles Wesley, "Come, Let Us Use the Grace Divine"

Do you promise, according to the grace given you,
to keep God's holy will and commandments
and walk in the same all the days of your life
as faithful members of Christ's holy church?

—Renunciation of Sin and Profession of Faith,
The United Methodist Hymnal

1. Searching the Scriptures

All scripture is inspired by God and is useful for teaching, for reproof, for correction, and for training in righteousness.

—2 Timothy 3:16

Whether the word be preached or read,
no saving benefit I gain
from empty sounds or letters dead;
unprofitable all and vain,
unless by faith thy word I hear
and see its heavenly character.

—Charles Wesley, "Whether the Word Be Preached or Read"

Reading the Bible as Scripture has less to do with what tools we bring to the task, however important these may be, and more to do with our own dispositions as we come to our engagement with Scripture. We come not to retrieve facts or to gain information, but to be formed. Scripture does not present us with texts to be mastered but with a Word—God's Word—intent of mastering us and shaping our lives.

—Joel B. Green

Scripture As a Means of Grace

In his sermon "The Means of Grace," Wesley identifies searching the Scriptures as an ordinary channel of God's grace. Grounded in the command of Jesus, "search the scriptures . . . it is they that testify on my behalf" (John 5:39), searching the Scriptures provided the means by which the Methodists measured belief ("found the grace of God") and practice ("thoroughly furnished unto all good works").[1] Wesley insisted that "under the general term of 'searching the Scriptures' both hearing, reading, and meditating are contained,"[2] and he gave specific guidance about this essential Christian practice:

> Would it not be advisable, (1.) To set apart a little time, if you can, every morning and evening, for that purpose? (2.) At each time, if you have leisure, to read a chapter out of the Old, and one of the New, Testament; if you cannot do this, to take a single chapter or a part of one? (3.) To read this with a single eye, to know the whole will of God, and a fixed resolution to do it? In order to know this will, you should (4.) Have a constant eye to the analogy of faith, the connexion and harmony there is between those grand, fundamental doctrines, original sin, justification by faith, the new birth, inward and outward holiness: (5.) Serious and earnest prayer should be constantly used before we consult the oracles of God . . . (6.) It might also be of use, if, while we read, we were frequently to pause, and examine ourselves by what we read, both with regard to our hearts and our lives.[3]

A close reading of Wesley's reflection on Scripture is revealing in its shaping of practice:

- Many Christians, throughout history, have discovered that *morning* and *evening* are the critical times for the reading of Scripture. These times can be the quietest moments of the day, free of the distractions of work and family. The morning can also be a time to read Scripture as a lens through which to see all that is scheduled for that day. The evening can be a time to reflect on all that has happened. In the morning we praise God and we ask for guidance, for insight, for strength. In the evening we read the Bible prayerfully, confessing our sin, giving thanks, remembering the works of the Lord. Individuals and small groups have found morning and evening to be appropriate times for the prayerful searching of Scripture. (See the orders for morning and evening prayer in the appendix of *The United Methodist Hymnal*.)
- Wesley urged the early Methodists to read the Old *and* the New Testaments. This of course is consistent with Christian

tradition, and an argument against those branches of Christianity that have ignored the Hebrew Scriptures (indeed this was the heresy of Marcionism in the early church). John Wesley insisted that "the Scripture, therefore, of the Old and New Testament, is a most solid and precious system of divine truth. Every part thereof is worthy of God; and all together are one entire body, wherein is no defect, no excess."[4] Those who have read through the whole of the Bible have learned that the Old and the New enrich and illumine each other.

- We read the Scriptures because we believe they contain the will and purpose of God for us. If we are to gain an understanding about the direction that our lives might take, the Bible is our most authoritative guide. Wesley then links understanding of the Scriptures with obedience, echoing the advice given to the early Christians from the letter of James: "Be doers of the word, and not merely hearers who deceive themselves" (James 1:22).

- By searching the Scriptures we discover the movement of God's grace in our lives. We see ourselves, in Wesley's words, when we are walking in darkness as God's people on a journey of self-recognition (that we are sinners), toward repentance,[5] and then to faith, acceptance of God's gift of regeneration and new birth, in the words of Albert Outler, "the beginning of the actual restoration of the *imago Dei*."[6] We are then still engaged in a dynamic process toward sanctification, the love of God (inward holiness) joined together with the love of neighbor (outward holiness), an experience of "grace-filled love that helps us become human and that nourishes our humanity."[7]

The Importance of Teachers and Mentors

Searching the Scriptures is much more than mastery of content or information. This practice is the process of "hearing, reading, and meditating" by which the Christian experiences "*reproof, . . . correction, and . . . training in righteousness*" (2 Timothy 3:16); thus this practice leads to transformation, which is a by-product of self-examination. The pastoral epistles in the New Testament

(1 and 2 Timothy and Titus) gave a clear priority to the importance of teaching the faith and stressed the authority and responsibility such a task entailed (1 Timothy 4, 6; 2 Timothy 1, 4; Titus 2). In this way searching the Scripture is a "socially embodied" practice, and never an exclusively private or individual exercise.

Phillip met Jesus in the Galilee and responded to his invitation: "Follow me" (John 1:43). Much had happened since that encounter. Jesus the Messiah had taught the disciples, healed the sick, fed the multitudes, and proclaimed God's kingdom. He had opened the Scriptures to those who would listen. He saw in his own life the fulfillment of Isaiah's prophecy, and he was crucified. His resurrection had empowered his disciples to tell his story, and this movement was further confirmed by the gift of God's spirit, a gift so explosive that it began to find receptivity among the Gentiles.

Phillip is now on the way from Jerusalem to Gaza, and he has another encounter. An Ethiopian official is reading from the book of the prophet Isaiah, and Phillip, perhaps in amazement, asks the question, "Do you understand what you are reading?" The Ethiopian responds, "How can I, unless someone guides me?" (Acts 8:31).

God speaks to us through the Scriptures, but God also places us within communities and traditions that help us interpret the Scriptures. This is a core conviction of Methodists, that *we read the Scriptures within a particular tradition*. Phillip had been with Jesus the Rabbi. He knew the life story of Jesus. He also knew the stories that shaped the life of Jesus. He saw himself within the ongoing story of what Jesus was doing in the world. Jesus had commanded his disciples to make other disciples (Matthew 28:18-20), and Phillip leads the Ethiopian eunuch into an experience of faith through baptism.

Sometimes an inner voice speaks to us, in the silence, and asks: *"Do you understand what you are reading?"* And we know that any understanding that we possess has come through guides, faithful men and women, past and present: Sunday school teachers, grandparents, preachers, professors, and friends. Because of them we are a part of the ongoing story of Jesus. For John and Charles Wesley, the primary mentor in the faith was surely their mother, Susanna, who spent time with each of her children each week in spiritual guidance, and who taught them to read, as five-year-olds, beginning with Genesis 1:1! The relationship of John and Charles is surely an echo of the relationship that Paul speaks of in his letter to Timothy: "I am reminded of your sincere faith, a faith that lived first in your grandmother Lois and your mother Eunice and now, I am sure, lives in you" (2 Timothy 1:5).

The apostolic tradition is the continuing witness of Scripture, passed from generation to generation, from Jesus to Phillip to the Ethiopian eunuch, from Lois to Eunice to Timothy, from Susanna Wesley to Charles and John, from those who have preached the gospel and taught the Scriptures in our own time. None of us reads the Bible in a vacuum.[8]

FOR REFLECTION: GIVE THANKS FOR THOSE WHO HAVE GUIDED YOU TOWARD AN UNDERSTANDING OF THE SCRIPTURES.

"When Have the Scriptures "come alive" for You"

Searching the Scripture on the Way to Emmaus

Another vivid example of searching the Scripture as a spiritual practice is found in Luke 24:13-35 ("The Walk to Emmaus"). I invite you to read this passage, and then to consider the following possibilities:

- Sometimes Jesus is traveling with us and we are not aware that he is there—we may not always be the best judge of what is going on spiritually.
- Sometimes Jesus has been with us in the past and we didn't recognize him—we were looking for something else, or the wrong thing.
- Wonderful things happen when we tell the story and break the bread. And that is what authentic worship is— Scripture, preaching, communion, fellowship.
- The disciples begin in despair and depression (at least discouragement). It is normal for all of us to have those times. Indeed, these experiences are common in the lives of maturing Christians, including John Wesley.
- The disciples want to give up, they are walking away, they have put their hopes in something that didn't pan out.
- They thought the cross was a sign of defeat. They will learn that the cross is a sign of victory.

- When the bread is broken their eyes are opened. God gives this moment to them, but it is a surprise. They discover the surprise in walking with Jesus.
- The disciples discover the surprise in a small group—only three people. Some of the best things happen when two or three are together—not always in gigantic gatherings.
- Then Jesus vanishes from their sight. Which means, maybe, that we are not always going to have spiritual highs, times when Jesus seems right beside us. But we know that he has been there.
- After they have the experience, they tell others about it. This is testimony. Resurrection living is so joyful that we cannot contain it.

Now reflect on these questions:

- Have you ever wanted to give up, walk away, because you had put your hopes in something that didn't pan out?
- Does reading the Emmaus story lead you toward exploration of a spiritual practice? Perhaps more frequent communion or testimony?
- How are several spiritual practices present in this passage?
- Does the story help you make sense of your own spiritual journey?
- Can you recall a time when your eyes were opened?

In searching the Scriptures, we recognize ourselves. God communes with us. God places us in communities of interpretation, where men and women help us toward greater understanding. And the practice of searching the Scriptures leads us to undertake other spiritual practices: testimony, communion, prayer.

A Man of One Book

John Wesley described himself as a "man of one book." By this he did not mean that he read only one book—in fact he read widely, across a number of disciplines. He was saying something else—that this book, the Bible, shaped his reading of all other books, and was thus worthy of a disciplined searching for truth and grace. This practice, as a vital element in the way of life that is Methodism, is threatened in two ways: by those whose reading of the Scripture is individualistic (rather than communal), ahistorical (apart from a living tradition), and abstract (divorced from concrete participation in mission), on the one hand; and by those who would discount the Scriptures as either culturally limited texts or teaching superseded by later received wisdom, on the other. Searching the Scriptures, as a spiritual practice, can threaten both conservatives and liberals who either use or misuse this resource as a weapon or ignore it, because the Scriptures always stand in judgment of us, searching us and setting the agenda for us. For this reason I find the Revised Common Lectionary, a scheduled pattern of reading, preaching, and teaching the Bible over three years, to be a helpful alternative to my own inclination to find scriptural passages that reinforce my own attitudes and perspectives! Those who have interpreted the Scriptures for us in imaginative ways have also enriched my spiritual life.[9]

Knowledge of Scripture is surely a beginning, but we must move beyond mere knowledge to practice—the integration of God's call and the human responses, listening and obedience. In this way we become "doers of the word." This movement will require:

- A regular discipline of reading in the Old and the New Testaments
- Communities and mentors who help us interpret the Scriptures
- Other practices that are woven together with the reading of Scripture
- Other persons who hold us accountable in helping the words become flesh

Transformation

My experience over the past ten years as a teacher or coteacher of *Disciple* Bible Study,[10] a thirty-four-week class, is that men and women who read approximately three-fourths of the Bible together are sometimes transformed. Participants see themselves in relationship to the God who makes a covenant with Israel.

They confess their own temptation to break covenant with God and to ignore the voices of the prophets. They sense the call of Jesus to becomes disciples, the fear and confusion associated with his death, and the amazement in the aftermath of his resurrection. They reflect on the expansion of the gospel to those who are outsiders, and they struggle with the issues facing the earliest churches, from sexuality to materialism to power. Finally, they engage in an exercise in which spiritual gifts are identified, and they share the Lord's Supper together, in a service based on John Wesley's covenant service.

While *Disciple* is an ecumenical study (it is never identified as United Methodist, and the scholars represent a range of traditions, including Jewish and Roman Catholic), its method can be traced back to this practice identified by Wesley as a means of grace. And the common experience of many participants is that the discipline of searching the Scriptures makes the experience of grace possible.

Participation in mission groups, or experience in particular life situations, can lead individuals to read the Scriptures in ways that were not obvious to them before. The poor in Latin America celebrate the Eucharist as a call upon God to feed the hungry, and the individual is led to see the poor as blessed and the rich as judged. A family member becomes ill in a way that carries a social stigma, and a reader of the Bible sees Samaritans in a new light. There is a job loss. An adult, for the first time, depends on the grace of others, and the New Testament doctrine takes on a new light. We do read the Scriptures out of our particular life settings—economic, geographical, gender, racial, social—and while exposure to interpretations that come from beyond our own perspectives can be upsetting, they also lead us into the deeper truths of the gospel.

Transformation often arises as we undertake inward and outward journeys: closer and more disciplined and prayerful reading of the Bible, and intentional involvement in the needs of the world. The genius of John Wesley can be understood in part by his love for the Bible ("a man of one book") and his insistence that Christianity is "essentially a social religion." We have failed if the Bible keeps us from engagement with the world, and we are lost if our engagement with the world is not grounded in the practice of searching the Scriptures.

2. Generosity with the Poor

Blessed are you who are poor, for yours is the kingdom of God.

—Luke 6:20

O that God would stir up the hearts of all that believe themselves his children, to evidence it by showing mercy to the poor!

—John Wesley

Wesley's specific admonitions about the spiritual benefits of saving and giving and about the spiritual hazards of frivolous spending are prophetic to the affluent, consumerist cultures, in which many of us live.

—Rebekah Miles

The poor were at the heart of John Wesley's ministry and theology. The Methodist movement began among the poor of eighteenth-century England. And yet relationship to the poor, and generosity toward them was a struggle for the Methodists from the beginning. Bishop Kenneth Carder, in reflecting on John Wesley's sermon "Causes of the Inefficacy of Christianity," has noted that:

> The Christian gospel has within it the seeds of ineffectiveness. Christian faith leads to diligence and frugality, which in turn often result in wealth and worldly success. Wealth and success then lead to the presumption of self-sufficiency and independence. In other words, affluence and success made the early Methodists less responsive to the gospel of grace.[1]

The sermon itself, particularly its conclusion, echoes the warning of Paul to Timothy: "The love of money is the root of all kinds of evil, and in their eagerness to be rich some have wandered away from the faith and pierced themselves with many pains" (1 Timothy 6:10).

What practices could sustain relationships with the poor and generosity toward them? The rules of the United Societies, formulated by John Wesley in 1739 for those "who appeared to be deeply convinced of sin and earnestly groaning for redemption," included the expectation of "doing good, by being in every kind merciful after their power; as they have opportunity, doing good of every possible sort, and, as far as possible, to all men."[2] David Lowes Watson notes that basic acts of compassion are located prior to the means of grace in the General Rules.[3] These practices were best carried out within class meetings, gatherings of Christians for the purpose of mutual accountability. Indeed the class meeting was a kind of laboratory for the relationship between doctrine and discipline, and in our own time many find Christian community to be a necessary context for spiritual resistance to the messages of our economic culture.

The Poor Receive Good News

Not only was generosity to the poor a part of the corporate and institutional life of the early Methodists, but also it was at the core of the church's proclamation. Again, Kenneth Carder's commentary is illuminating:

> Wesley's preaching elicited the most positive response among the poor and marginalized. His message of universal redemption and sufficient grace in all and irresistible grace in none opened the door for men and women who had been marginalized by eighteenth-century English society. . . . Exploitation and deprivation stripped them of dignity and self-respect and many escaped in drunkenness and sensuality. Wesley went among the new underclass, warned of the judgment of God and proclaimed a gospel of justifying grace which bears fruit in holy living. He gathered those who responded to the gospel of grace into new groups in which each person found acceptance, a new sense of dignity, and a community which held them accountable. . . . Wesley planted the Methodist societies in pockets of

poverty and nourished them with the gospel of justifying and sanctifying grace.[4]

Generosity to the poor was a part of Wesley's practice in his proclamation, in his missionary activity, and in his ordering of the life of the church. These practices were deeply rooted in his theology of grace and its congruence with a practice of generosity with the poor. Theodore Jennings suggests that the development of this practice was at the heart of the shift in Wesley's ministry, and is the key, to a greater degree than the Aldersgate experience, in understanding Wesley's life: "This vocational crisis was resolved only when Wesley discovered a new vocation, one that was to energize him for another half century and more: that of evangelist to the poor and disinherited of England."[5]

A Church Among the Poor

A few years ago I participated in the beginning of an ongoing relationship between a North American congregation and the Evangelical Methodist Church of Bolivia. Our orientation was led by a former missionary to that country who had served primarily in the field of health care. When the Methodist Church was allowed by the government of that country to begin mission work, in the early twentieth century, it was exclusively in health care and education. The educational strategy was to educate the elite children and young people of Bolivia, with the hope that such a mission would benefit the lives of the larger society. Two schools, the Institutos Americanos, one in La Paz, the capital city, and another in Cochabamba, were established, and over a period of fifty years they had trained many of the leaders of Bolivia, including presidents and cabinet officials. Yet most missionaries and most Bolivian Methodists concluded that such a strategy had effected little change in the church and in the society. And so an alternative strategy was developed, in which the focus would be on the poor and on the local congregations in which they were a part. The result was the renewal of Methodism in Bolivia. Today almost 1.4 million people identify themselves as Methodists in Latin America and the Caribbean.

For me, this seems almost to be a modern-day parable of Wesley's movement in eighteenth-century England. Many also

"A Bout Schmidt"

see the United Methodists Bishops' Initiative on Children and Poverty (1996) within this same tradition.

The Danger of Riches

A final word about generosity with the poor. One of the most quoted statements by Wesley comes in an essay written near the end of his life, entitled "Thoughts Upon Methodism": "I am not afraid that the people called Methodists should ever cease to exist either in Europe or America. But I am afraid, lest they should only exist as a dead sect, having the form of religion without the power."[6]

How might we become a "dead sect," exhibiting "faith without works" (James 2:26)? Wesley continues in the same essay: "It nearly concerns us to understand how the case stands with us at present. I fear, wherever riches have increased, (exceeding few are the exceptions,) the essence of religion, the mind that was in Christ, has decreased in the same proportion."[7]

Where generosity with the poor is practiced, our early Methodist experience should teach us, there is a correspondence with an understanding of graced human nature. The poor are able to hear a message of grace, apart from works, as good news. *The poor can teach us to understand our doctrinal heritage!* Kenneth L. Carder's assertion is both prophetic and liberating:

> The poor, therefore, were not only the beneficiaries of Wesley's proclamation of grace, they were channels of that grace to Wesley. The poor and marginalized helped to shape the central theme of his preaching: God's prevenient, justifying, and sanctifying grace which transforms individuals and societies.[8]

For those who serve in settings "where riches have increased," Wesley's preaching and teaching on this subject is rich in its treatment of the various New Testament traditions. The moral theologian Sondra Ely Wheeler has identified a variety of perspectives on money and wealth in the New Testament, and these have found expression in Methodist practice:

- Wealth can be a stumbling block (see Wesley's "Thoughts Upon Methodism").

- Wealth can be a competing object of devotion (see Wesley's reflection on Jesus' insistence that "where your treasure is, there will your heart will be also" in Matthew 6:21).[9]
- Wealth can be a resource for human needs (see Wesley's sermon "The Use of Money").[10]

From Greed to Generosity

A great deal of my ministry has been carried out among folks who are pursuing the good life, and yet, at times someone will take a deep breath and make a confession to me: *The good life is killing us.* We are the most prosperous and the most violent culture in the world. We are the most affluent and the most medicated culture in the world. We are the most professing Christian culture in the world. We are the most anxious culture in the world. We engage in "patterns of mutual self-destruction."[11] The good life is killing us.

We have a great deal, but we want more. The seven deadly sins— pride, envy, anger, apathy, lust, gluttony, and greed—are as ancient as the Scriptures and the early church, and as relevant as last night's television news and this morning's newspaper. Greed affects *politics,* selling pardons for money and nature preserves for corporate gain. Greed affects the *church.* The American church is often caught up, to a great degree, in worldly success. One participant/observer in American religious life has said that we count "bodies, bucks, and buildings"! And a veteran evangelical missionary commented, "If we counted the number of reported conversions since the end of World War II in Japan, we would have more Christians than people." Greed also affects *families,* when there are corporate takeovers and questionable strategies and workaholic behavior patterns.[12]

Greed has been incorrectly equated with money. First Timothy 6:10 reads "The *love* of money is the root of all evil." It is not true that "money is the root of all evil." The *love* of money is the root of all evil. Who doesn't love money? And yet, I think of that confession: the good life is killing us.

As North American Methodist Christians, we struggle with money and greed. And in so doing we may ask the question: How can we overcome this deadly sin? Money has a light side and a dark side. Money can be a blessing and a curse. Money can wound, and money can heal. Money can change a person's life. Some members of our congregation are helping to fund the education of a young adult in Guatemala. In Guatemala, many rural children either go to school, or make their way to Guatemala City, where they are taken advantage of in many destructive ways. A few people in our church are sending a young woman to school. It is not a great deal of money, but it changes her life. Money can be a blessing.

And we have a lot of money. Our nation has a lot of money. Our churches have a lot of money. We individually have a lot of money. Compared to the masses of people on this planet, we have a lot of money. You would think that would be the good life. But the good life is killing us. Money can also separate people, when it is withheld or used as a weapon. In the Sermon on the Mount, one of John Wesley's favorite portions of the Scripture, Jesus teaches about money and faith, money and witness. Later in the Gospel of Matthew, Jesus speaks more specifically about witness: "Everyone therefore who acknowledges me before others, I also will acknowledge before my Father in heaven" (Matthew 10:32).

It is about profession of faith. When we profess faith in Jesus we know that our security is in him. And this is an argument with the status quo: our ultimate security is not found in many of the likely contenders that pervade our lives.

- Our security is not in the *stock market*. The stock market goes up and down.
- Our security is not in the *government*. Governments rise and fall.
- Our security is not in the *company*. Companies split and merge and restructure.
- Our security is not in the *family*. Families break apart and do harm to each other.
- Our security is in Jesus.

FOR REFLECTION: LOCATE A HYMNAL AND THUMB THROUGH IT UNTIL YOU FIND A HYMN THAT FOCUSES ON SECURITY AND TRUST IN JESUS.

Jesus must have known that money could become our source of security, even an idol, because he said, "You can't worship God and Money both" (Matthew 6 *THE MESSAGE*). Worshiping money, thinking about money, obsessing about money, leads us down the wrong path. Don't worry about your life, Jesus says, God will take care of you. God takes care of the wildflowers; God will take care of you.

The good life has led us down the path of anxiety: anxiety about the present, anxiety about the future, anxiety about our possessions, anxiety about our wealth. And because we have become anxious we are tempted *not* to see God's abundance. Eugene Peterson's translation in *The Message* is compelling:

> What I'm trying to do here is to get you to relax, to not be so preoccupied with *getting* so you can respond to God's *giving*. . . . Steep your life in God-reality, God-initiative, God-provisions. Don't worry about missing out. You'll find all your everyday human concerns will be met. (Matthew 6)

At times we envision a world of scarcity. Scarcity produces greed. Scarcity leads to the false belief that there is not enough.

- When we do not see the abundance, we do not see God.
- When we do not live by faith, we become anxious.
- When we live with a misplaced security, we forget that God will take care of us.
- When we lose touch with the doctrine of providence, we forget that his eye is on the sparrow.
- When our priorities are skewed, we forget to seek first the kingdom of God and his righteousness.

And at this point the deadly sin of greed creeps into our lives. Greed happens when money takes the place of God. Greed happens when we neglect the poor. Greed happens when we are defined by our money. But money doesn't define us. Perry Ainsworth, who ministered at the Wesley Chapel in Birmingham, England at the beginning of the twentieth century, insisted that "the rich are saved in spite of their riches and not by means of them. Jesus saw that the more we have of the things that are seen, the less likely we are to realize our need of the unseen things."[13]

Money is not our source of security. Money does not define who we are. But money is strongly connected to the Christian faith. Money was a great concern of Jesus. He spoke about money more than any subject, except the kingdom of God. And money was of great concern to John Wesley.

The Methodist movement grew from five people to fifty thousand during the eighteenth century in England. Methodists built schools, lending agencies for the poor, pharmacies, and homes for the aged. On August 4, 1786, John Wesley was near the end of his life. He had taken a tour of Britain, and he was discouraged. Note again the meaning of his journal: "I am not afraid that we as Methodists will cease to exist. I am afraid that we become a dead church, having the form of God without the power of God. I am concerned that we have become affluent, and that we no longer have a desire to give to those in need."[14]

Wesley practiced what he preached. As a student and teacher at Oxford he lived on twenty-eight pounds a year, and he gave two pounds to God. Later in life, when he earned 120 pounds, he gave away ninety-two pounds. He said that if at his death he had more than ten pounds to his name he could be called a robber. At his funeral, 6 paupers carried him to his grave. Each was paid one pound, thus depleting his resources. Wesley earned about as much money as any private citizen in eighteenth-century England. He preached a famous sermon entitled "On the Use of Money." Like all good sermons it had three points. "Make all you can, save all you can, give all you can."

In his sermon Wesley gave specific instructions about how the early Methodists were to make money and save money. There were parameters to making and saving money morally, spiritually, and physically.

- Moral boundaries guide us to consider the ethical implications of the work that we do.
- Spiritual boundaries help us discover the will of God in our vocational lives.
- Physical boundaries remind us of the limitations of our bodies and the need for rest.

FOR REFLECTION: HAVE YOU CONSIDERED THESE BOUNDARIES IN THE WORK THAT YOU DO AND THE INCOME THAT IS PRODUCED BY YOUR WORK? IN YOUR EXPERIENCE, HOW DO METHODISTS PRACTICE GENEROSITY WITH THE POOR?

In the call to "give all you can," he gave us a practice that moves us from *greed to generosity*. It seems to me that in Wesley's sermon we find the clue to overcoming the sin of greed. It is a movement from greed to generosity. It is the way that leads to life.

A Parable

Occasionally life brings a parable to us. One day I encountered two people in our congregation. One was a woman who, at least externally, has every advantage our culture affords. She blew into my office to complain about something. She did not actually want to do anything constructive. She was too busy. Some program of the church did not meet her standards. We walked out into the parking lot together, and she got into her late model, large vehicle and drove away.

Later that day I encountered another woman in our church. She lives a very simple life, with none of the trappings of affluence that surround many. She was loading gifts for the Angel Tree, a Christmas ministry with children, into her car. I would guess that her car is at least 15 years old, maybe older. I would also guess that she was providing gifts not just for one child, but for several children. There was a big smile on her face as she shoved everything into the car and left the parking lot.

In that parable, who do you think was living the good life? And who do you think was a part of a spiritual practice? We overcome the deadly sin in the movement from greed to generosity. A lot of money will pass through our lives and bank accounts in our lifetimes. Many among the people called Methodists have heard the first two points in Wesley's sermon: Make all you can. Save all you can. The third point is the most difficult: Give all you can.

- How do we witness through the use of our money?
- How do we profess faith and trust in Jesus through our money?
- How do we practice generosity with the poor?

God has not given us a lot of money so that we might worry about it, or hoard it, or let it rule our lives. God has given us a lot of money so that we might give it away. Listen to the teaching of Jesus and the guidance of John Wesley:

- Do not worry about what you will eat or drink or wear. The Gentiles strive for such things, and your heavenly Father knows that you need them (see Matthew 6). God will provide.
- Seek the kingdom of God and his righteousness, and these things will be added to you (see Matthew 6). Invest in the things that are eternal.
- Make all you can, save all you can, give all you can (Wesley). Move from greed to generosity.
- Blessed are the poor (see Luke 6:20). Experience the grace of Jesus Christ.

3. Testimony

You will be my witnesses in Jerusalem, in all Judea and Samaria, and to the ends of the earth.

—Acts 1:8

He breaks the power of cancelled sin,
he sets the prisoner free;
his blood can make the foulest clean;
his blood availed for me.

—Charles Wesley, "O For a Thousand Tongues to Sing"

What matters is that the gospel be appropriately presented. The message should be heralded boldly and clearly, and it should remain true to the fundamental content of the gospel. Thus it focuses on what God has done in Christ, on the offers of forgiveness and the gift of the Holy Spirit, and on the need for repentance. If what is preached is something other than the content of the gospel, say, a string of stories about religious experiences or a promise of health and wealth in return for personal and financial commitment, then evangelism has not occurred.

—William J. Abraham

These are his last words, these words of Jesus. He says, "You will be my witnesses." We pay close attention to the last words of those we love. I have sat with families, as we have prayed, and then I have been silent and listened. Last words are important. Jesus in Acts 1:8 gives his last great commandment: "You will be my witnesses." Witness is important; important enough to be the last thing Jesus would say to us. How is witness (or testimony) a basic spiritual practice? I will focus on three questions: *What* is witness? *Why* do we witness? And *how* do we witness?

Speaking the Truth

God chose you "in order that you may proclaim the mighty acts of him who called you out of darkness into his marvelous light" (1 Peter 2:9). Another translation has it, you are "God's instruments to do his work and speak out for him to tell others of the night and day difference he made for you" *(THE MESSAGE)*.

What is witness? A witness is someone who speaks the truth. We speak honestly about ourselves to God. We confess our need for mercy, for forgiveness, for grace. God knows us better than we know ourselves. We do not need to pretend before God. A part of our witness is our own honesty before God. Another part of our witness is speaking honestly to others *about* God.

I have a friend who runs a small business with his wife. At times they do well, at other times they struggle. Most of the time, it seems, they live with a lot of stress. Those who operate small businesses probably know what I mean. They have a few employees, usually about five, and my friend took a special interest in one of them. This employee was a young man with great potential. They had a good working relationship that blossomed into a friendship. My friend shared with me that he felt a desire, a calling even, to share his faith with his employee. He said, "I don't want to scare him, I don't want to come across as arrogant, I don't want to judge him, but I do want to share what is important to me—my faith in Jesus Christ—with him." And so he took his friend to dinner one evening and he did just that. He gave thanks for their friendship, they enjoyed the meal together, and then he said, "If you are going to know the real me, you need to know about my faith. I am a Christian." Witness is:

- Speaking the truth about ourselves to God
- Speaking the truth about God to others

In a trial, the witness is of tremendous importance. The witness stands, takes an oath, and answers questions in a very specific way. The witness speaks honestly and truthfully. This practice is a complex one in our own culture. Political and ecclesiastical leaders at the highest level have given false testimony, at times under oath. Others have sought to divorce the public and private spheres, drawing a line that separates the personal and corporate. For this reason, testimony must always be shared alongside other practices, which together add up to a way of life.

If we are to be faithful witnesses for Jesus Christ, we must see the importance of speaking honestly about ourselves to God, and about God to others. I am talking about *verbal* witness to the mercy of God through Jesus Christ. Do you know the song, "They Will Know We Are Christians by Our Love"? I like that song, I grew up singing it, but I chuckled when a friend commented about that title, "They will know we are Christians by our love—on a good day, maybe!" They will know we are Christians by our witness.

The Experience of Grace

But this leads to a deeper question: why witness? The earliest Christians were compelled to bear witness to something that had shaped their life together. They were not primarily seeking to advance an argument against a competing philosophy. Instead, the first believers were simply attempting to make sense of something miraculous that had occurred in their midst:

> We declare to you what was from the beginning, what we have heard, what we have seen with our eyes, what we have looked at and touched with our hands, concerning the word of life— this life was revealed, and we have seen it and testify to it. . . . This is the message we have heard from him and proclaim to you, that God is light and in him is no darkness at all. (1 John 1:1-2, 5)

We bear witness to miracles. Some we hear with our own ears— the spoken word of forgiveness and reconciliation. Some we see with our own eyes—the transformation of a human life. Some we touch with our own hands—the birth of a child. It is a miracle when we are transformed from darkness to light. This revelation makes our witness both possible and necessary. "We cannot hide the light under a bushel," we sang as children, echoing the teaching of Jesus in the Sermon on the Mount (Matthew 5:15). We have to let it shine!

FOR REFLECTION: CAN YOU THINK ABOUT A POSITIVE EXPERIENCE YOU'VE HAD LATELY AS A CHRISTIAN? CAN YOU DISCOVER A WAY TO SHARE THAT EXPERIENCE?

Jesus said, "You will be my witnesses." He chose ordinary people like you and me to be witnesses. We are sinners. We have the treasure of the gospel in earthen vessels (2 Corinthians 4). But maybe because of our imperfections, our sin, we have become silent. We think, maybe this isn't worth talking about, or maybe I shouldn't be the one doing the talking. And so we keep the secret to ourselves.

But Jesus said, "You will be my witnesses." I am a parent of two children. I am sensitive to messages in the media. I saw a billboard the other day of a boy and a girl. "If you don't talk to them about sex," it read, "someone else will." That is also true about the faith. If we don't talk to our children, whether they are five or fifteen or fifty, about the faith, someone else will.

To talk about our faith is to witness. Why witness? Because, in Jesus Christ, God has touched our lives with amazing grace. And that is worth talking about.

A Circle of Witness

We've touched on what witness is, and why we witness. But *how* do we do it? The people to whom we are most likely to be effective witnesses in our lives are a small circle of ten to twelve people: family, close friends, coworkers. This is our circle of witness. These persons are the ones with whom we need to share the story, the old, old story, as the hymn says, of Jesus and his love. They need to know what has happened in our lives. They need to know our testimony. We need to be honest with them. Here it helps if we place witness in the context of other basic spiritual practices:

- As we witness we are also *listening to the Scriptures.*
- As we witness we are also *giving thanks and praise to God.*[1]

- As we witness we are also *practicing hospitality.*
- As we witness we sometimes find ourselves *extending grace to the poor and receiving grace from them.*

I invite you to consider a spiritual exercise. Write down the name of one person in your closest circle of ten to twelve people. I want you to prepare to be a witness to them. You will want to pray about that person, and then, in love, you'll want to be as honest as you can with them in your witness.

Getting Clarity About Witness

What is witness? Witness is proclaiming the mighty acts of God, who called us out of darkness into his marvelous light. Witness is not good advice about what you ought to do with your life. Witness is good *news.* It is the anonymous prayer:

> Lord, I'm not what I *want* to be.
> Lord, I'm not what I'm *going* to be,
> But by your grace, Lord,
> I'm not what I *used* to be.

Why should we witness? Because God has touched our lives with amazing grace. Maybe we have been forgiven, maybe we have been healed, maybe we have been restored, maybe we have been cleansed, maybe we have been set free, maybe we have been given a second chance in life, maybe we have made that journey from darkness into light and we are not where we want to be, and we are not where we are going to be, but we are not where we used to be.

How do we witness? We become more and more honest about whom we are before God, and we become more and more honest and transparent with others, especially those closest to us, about whom God is to us.

A Tradition of Testimony

Witness is a form of *testimony.* Thomas Hoyt Jr. defines the practice of testimony in the following way: "We borrow from the world of courtrooms and trials when we talk about 'testimony.'

Testimony occurs in particular settings—a courtroom or a church—where a community expects to hear the truth spoken."[2]

Undoubtedly the most prominent example of testimony or witness in our tradition was that of John Wesley himself, reflecting on an experience at a meeting on Aldersgate Street in London.[3] Albert Outler is correct in his assertion that "this is easily the most familiar passage in all Wesley's writings. In the Methodist tradition, it stands as the equivalent of Paul's experience on the Damascus road and Augustine's conversion in the Milanese garden."[4] Here is Wesley's account of Wednesday, May 24, 1738:

> In the evening I went very unwillingly to a society in Aldersgate Street, where one was reading Luther's Preface to the Epistle to the Romans. About a quarter before nine, while he was describing the change that God works in the heart through faith in Christ, I felt my heart strangely warmed. I felt I did trust in Christ, Christ alone for salvation; and an assurance was given me that he had taken away *my* sins, even *mine*, and saved *me* from the law of sin and death.[5]

Wesley's testimony of what happened at Aldersgate has elicited a variety of responses from his followers. Several scholars offered appraisals of the meaning of this testimony in 1988, the 250th anniversary of Aldersgate. Two reflections given by Roberta Bondi and David Watson express reservations about our common interpretation of Aldersgate. Bondi acknowledges that it has been a "sacred event for United Methodists" and yet at the same time argues that the effects of an "Aldersgate spirituality" are "very destructive."[6] She bases this judgment on two accounts: first, an Aldersgate spirituality ignores the complexity of human life, and describes an end point of the Christian life that cannot be experienced at its beginning; and second, she suggests that "deep attitudes of the heart" come "a little at a time through a long process of practice, prayer, training, and, especially, God's grace."[7]

Again, pastors will sense this as having been confirmed in parish experience. The great exception is the person who has an instantaneous life-transforming experience; the more common experience is found in ongoing spiritual practices that bring about growth in grace over time. And most pastors will also have had the experience of listening to individuals who are discouraged because they have not had "Aldersgate-type" experiences that have brought assurance and inner peace. Life is usually more complex than that. And indeed, this seemed to have been the case with John Wesley. As Albert Outler again notes, "in the first six months after 'Aldersgate' he reports numerous instances of acute spiritual depression, equal in severity to anything preceding."[8] David Watson argues that Aldersgate was a powerful affirmation of the works of piety in a Christian life, but then he insists, "if we interpret that moment of illumination and assurance 250 years ago as both the power and the form of our Christian discipleship" we commit a serious error. The experience might serve as the power of Christian discipleship, but that is therefore "only half of the equation." The "form of Christian discipleship, which he was always at pains to stress as concomitant with the power, was that which would either render grace effectual in a Christian's life, or would quench it."[9]

Testimony and the Practices

I find both Bondi and Watson to be persuasive, regarding our evaluation of Wesley's testimony about Aldersgate, and yet there is a broader context to the experience. Wesley notes in his journals preceding the experience that he had been reading the New Testament; he attended worship at Saint Paul's Cathedral in London, where the anthem was taken from Psalm 130 ("Out of the depths have I cried unto thee, O LORD," KJV); he gave spiritual direction; he fasted, and took Holy Communion as often as possible. It could be that his experience at Aldersgate is best interpreted within the frame of these additional practices. Its limitation is that it does not, at least in the form in which it is given in our tradition, adequately expose the surrounding practices that both make the experience possible and help sustain it. As Craig Dykstra has noted, "participating in the disciplines of the church does not bring about or cause faith or growth in the life of faith. Rather, engagement in the church's practices puts us in a position where we may recognize and participate in God's grace in the world."[10]

The power of Wesley's testimony is that it conveys the grace of God that comes to us as a gift. Martin Luther, the great reformer of Christianity, argued that Psalm 130 taught the basic truth of the gospel. He preached a sermon on this psalm, and in it he said, "With God alone is forgiveness. If anyone wants to amount to something before God, he must insist on *grace*, not merit."[11]

The evening John Wesley heard Psalm 130 performed as an anthem in Saint Paul's Cathedral in London, he went to a room on Aldersgate Street and he experienced the gospel, in which his heart was strangely warmed by the grace of God.

Testimony, Confession, and Grace

A part of Wesley's experience is common to many of us. When we hit bottom, there is a firm foundation. There is forgiveness and grace. At times this is our witness, our testimony. If the Lord should mark iniquities, the psalmist asks, who could stand? The answer: no one. We are saved by grace alone! My friend Anthony Robinson has written in compelling ways about his pastoral experience. He went into a deep depression that lasted a couple of years. He had no idea why he felt so debilitated and overwhelmed. But in his recovery he came to a conclusion: "I . . . had turned a religion of grace into a religion of good works and achievement."[12]

Many pastors and church leaders would admit, if we are honest, that we have turned a religion of grace into a religion of good works. And sometimes, by God's grace, we have hit bottom in some way—a spiritual crisis, an intervention by someone, a health matter. Christian practices may arise out of the wrong motivations, or we may have become immobilized by the realization that our faith and our practice have become disconnected. And our practices can be rooted in a false understanding of the nature of God.[13]

FOR REFLECTION: HAVE YOU EVER THOUGHT, DEEP IN YOUR GUT, THAT IF YOU WERE JUST A BETTER PERSON GOD WOULD LOVE YOU MORE?

If you've hit bottom, this can be an enslaving thought: that you can become more loved by God by being a better person. But listen to the Scripture that spoke to John Wesley just prior to one of his most powerful spiritual experiences: "If you, O LORD, should mark iniquities, Lord, who could stand? But there is forgiveness with you."

The testimony of Psalm 130 is that there is forgiveness; there is grace, a way out, a way up. This was the testimony of the apostle Paul and the founders of our faith, John and Charles Wesley. And this, by God's grace, is our testimony. Serene Jones offers a wonderful summary of the place of testimony among graced people:

> When one accepts the fact that one does not have to earn the love of God, one cannot help but turn and offer praise and thanksgiving to the God who has bestowed this love. Further, in praising God, one desires to please God, not so that God might bestow more grace but rather that one might delight the God who has given the gift of life abundant.[14]

4. Singing

With gratitude in your hearts sing psalms, hymns, and spiritual songs to God.

—Colossians 3:16

Learn these tunes before you learn any others; afterwards, learn as many as you please.

—John Wesley, "Directions for Singing"

If music is the language of the soul made audible, then human voices, raised in concert in human gatherings, are primary instruments of the soul.

—Don Saliers

United Methodists and Singing

There are Christian practices that Methodists have done together over time, and some are more obvious than others. Methodists have been profoundly shaped by the hymns of Charles Wesley in singing their faith.[1] And Methodists have also shaped the theology and practice of other traditions most powerfully by the legacy of the Wesley hymns. I have lived through new methods of church school curriculum, modern scriptural translations, and revisions of hymnals. The latter, by far, has the greatest impact on the worshiping congregation. For many, theological claims about God, Jesus Christ, the Holy Spirit, the church, our vocational calling in the world, and human destiny are found most powerfully in the hymns of our faith. Indeed, Wesley described the early Methodist hymns as a "little body of experimental and practical divinity."[2]

Engagement with the practice of singing the hymns of our tradition can help us experience the fullness of the Christian faith, especially as we live by the liturgical calendar. This calendar helps us order our lives by the events in the life of Jesus: the anticipation of his birth, his birth, his baptism, his public ministry, his suffering, his death and resurrection, and his gift of the Spirit to the church. Without the liturgical year, we are at the mercy of cultural priorities that order our lives: sporting events, political drama, and consumer cycles. The liturgical year helps the church to maintain the integrity of the fullness of Christian faith and life. And the hymns of the Wesleyan tradition are a wonderful way to enter into the liturgical year as a spiritual practice.

Incarnation

One of the best-known hymns of Charles Wesley is "Hark! the Herald Angels Sing." Based upon the account of the birth of Jesus in Luke 2, this carol begins with the proclamation of the Savior (testimony), and witnesses to what happens through the gift of Jesus ("God and sinners reconciled"). The carol is strongly incarnational, as is evident in the third verse:

Hail the heaven born Prince of Peace!
Hail the Sun of Righteousness!
Light and life to all he brings,
risen with healing in his wings.
Mild he lays his glory by, born that we no more may die,
born to raise us from the earth, born to give us second birth.
Hark! the herald angels sing, "Glory to the newborn King!"[3]

In this one stanza and refrain of the beloved carol, there are echoes of Isaiah 9, John 1, and a number of other biblical passages. There is a rich gathering of metaphors for the work of God among us: peace, righteousness, light, life, healing, new birth. And there is a confidence in the promise and fulfillment that defines the Christmas season.

"Hark! the Herald Angels Sing" is both richly doctrinal ("offspring of a virgin's womb," "veiled in flesh the Godhead see") and thoroughly practical (an invitation to glorify Jesus Christ). It is a wonderful commentary about human nature and divine grace. And it is one of Christianity's best-loved carols!

Epiphany

The incarnation of God in the flesh flows into the experience of Epiphany, the manifestation of the light that will shine upon all peoples, beginning with the magi (Matthew 2:1-12). Charles Wesley's hymn "Christ Whose Glory Fills the Skies" is almost a continuation of the Christmas faith expressed in "Hark! the Herald Angels Sing." The light that shines upon the shepherds in Luke 2:9 cannot be contained in one time and place:

> Christ, whose glory fills the skies, Christ, the true, the only light,
> Sun of Righteousness, arise, triumph o'er the shades of night;
> Dayspring from on high, be near; Daystar, in my heart appear. [4]

While the Epiphany of the Lord (January 6) marks the conclusion of the Christmas season, it can also be understood as the logical extension of it. The glory of God in Jesus Christ is not only a private or personal experience; it will manifest itself in the public ministry of Jesus, which is affirmed at his baptism (Matthew 3; Luke 3) and again at his transfiguration (Matthew 17; Mark 9; Luke 9).

The season after the Epiphany can be a time for the church to focus on the practice of baptism (and the reaffirmation of the baptismal covenant). In the life of Jesus, and in the life of the disciple, remembrance of one's baptism can be a source of encouragement and hope. As the light shone upon Jesus at his baptism, we pray for a new epiphany:

> Visit then this soul of mine; pierce the gloom of sin and grief;
> fill me, Radiancy divine, scatter all my unbelief;
> more and more thyself display, shining to the perfect day.[5]

Passion

The incarnation of God, expressed in the life of Jesus, leads to passion. Charles Wesley composed a number of excellent passion texts. The hymn "And Can It Be?" expresses gratitude for participation in the cruciform life of Jesus:

> And can it be that I should gain an interest in the Savior's
> blood!
> Died he for me? who caused his pain! For me? who him to
> death pursued?
> Amazing love! How can it be that thou, my God, shouldst die
> for me? [6]

This gratitude takes the form of amazement and wonder:

> O Love divine, what hast thou done!
> The immortal God hath died for me!
> The Father's coeternal Son bore all my sins upon the tree.
> The immortal God for me hath died:
> My Lord, my Love is crucified! [7]

In another hymn, Charles Wesley gives more explicit reference to forgiveness and justification:

> 'Tis finished! All my guilt and pain,
> I want no sacrifice beside;
> for me, for me the Lamb is slain;
> 'Tis finished! I am justified. [8]

Each hymn describes the personal appropriation of the gift: note the repetition of the words "for me" in each of the three hymn texts. Any of the three might lead the worshiper into the depths of what it means to take up the cross. All echo the confession of the apostle Paul: "I have been crucified with Christ; and it is no longer I who live, but it is Christ who lives in me. And the life I now live in the flesh I live by faith in the Son of God, who loved me and gave himself for me" (Galatians 2:19-20).

Resurrection Life in the Power of the Spirit

The life and death of Jesus is followed by the miracle of resurrection, and thus at Easter we sing another hymn of Charles Wesley's:

65

Soar we now where Christ has led, Alleluia!
Following our exalted Head, Alleluia!
Made like him, like him we rise, Alleluia!
Ours the cross, the grave, the skies, Alleluia![9]

As human beings we share in the death and resurrection of Jesus. Our confession of faith is made possible by the presence of the Holy Spirit:

Spirit of faith, come down, reveal the things of God,
and make to us the Godhead known, and witness with the
blood. . . .
No one can truly say that Jesus is the Lord,
unless thou take the veil away and breathe the living Word.[10]

This is life in God's grace. And yet grace always leads us into service; profession of faith corresponds with practice of faith, and the power of the resurrection moves toward the restoration of creation:

To serve the present age, my calling to fulfill;
O may it all my powers engage to do my Master's will![11]

Advent

The liturgical year begins with anticipation of the coming of Jesus Christ, and is completed in the desire, never fully realized in this human pilgrimage, of the coming kingdom. Charles Wesley's Advent text carries within it a profound statement about the future of humanity:

Come, thou long-expected Jesus, born to set thy people free;
from our fears and sins release us, let us find our rest in thee. [12]

This Advent hymn is remarkable in several respects. S T Kimbrough has noted the historical context in Charles Wesley's encounter with the practice of human slavery in Charleston, South Carolina upon his return to England. The text is also an invitation to a number of Christian practices: forgiveness, sabbath, and generosity with the poor.

To Claim and Test Our Heritage

The Christian practice of singing hymns leads us to the awareness of "God's active presence for the life of the world."[13] In these eight hymns composed by Charles Wesley, one senses a vision of human nature and divine providence. There is a complex set of images that describe God's gift of grace and our human vocation as recipients of grace. And yet there is within our tradition a problem. Despite John Wesley's insistence that one should "learn these tunes before you learn any others; afterwards learn as many as you please,"[14] our singing is sometimes shaped by other streams of Christian tradition, from revivalist gospel to contemporary praise to social gospel, music that does not always possess the depth of doctrinal richness found in the writings of Charles Wesley. Some of the hymn supplements and songbooks of the last century included almost none of the Wesley hymns, and many congregations that have transitioned from traditional to contemporary forms of worship have lost touch with this practice as well. I am not suggesting a blanket indictment of non-Wesleyan hymns or praise choruses; I am simply suggesting that we test newer resources for worship in light of the music that has shaped our tradition for 250 years.

The loss of this body of practical divinity also threatens our unique contribution to the Christian movement. As Lester Ruth has noted, "The Wesleys' bifocal commitment to an evangelistic Word directed toward the world and to a gathered fellowship around the Table before God provides the proper balance. . . . With respect to worship, the Wesleys' legacy was the ability to hold things together."[15] The hymns of the early Methodists held together personal faith, corporate worship, generosity with the poor and witness in the world. These hymns were the sustained reflection of mature Christians who had searched the Scriptures and unearthed images, metaphors, and phrases that made plain the doctrines of the faith. A British Methodist pastor and composer of hymns, Fred Pratt Green, has done much to renew this practice. His hymn, "The Church of Christ in Every Age," serves as both example and guide to the important practice of singing our faith:

> The church of Christ, in every age beset by change but Spirit-
> led,

must claim and test its heritage and keep on rising from the
dead. . . .
We have no mission but to serve in full obedience to our Lord,
to care for all, without reserve, and spread his liberating word.[16]

An additional question that is always put to the practice of
singing is the correspondence between the words that we sing (or
speak) and the character of our lives. This was the critique of the
prophet of Israel:

> I hate, I despise your festivals, and I take no delight in your
> solemn assemblies. . . . Take away from me the noise of your
> songs; I will not listen to the melody of your harps. But let jus-
> tice roll down like waters, and righteousness like an everflow-
> ing stream. (Amos 5:21, 23-24)

A practice like singing, when placed alongside the other practices, adds up to a way of life. Otherwise, our music might
be nothing more than a "noisy gong or a clanging cymbal"
(1 Corinthians 13:1). Again, the words of contemporary Methodist
composer Fred Pratt Green help us to sing our faith:

> If our hearts are lifted where devotion soars
> high above this hungry, suffering world of ours,
> lest our hymns should drug us to forget its needs,
> forge our Christian worship into Christian deeds.[17]

5. Holy Communion

Do this in remembrance of me.

—Luke 22:19

Because thou hast said: "Do this for my sake," the mystical bread we gladly partake.

—Charles Wesley, "Because Thou Hast Said"

The open table with public sinners and outcasts was Jesus' major and most provocative proclamation of the new order of the kingdom.

—Mortimer Arias

The Meal

The meal is, of course, at the center of the biblical story. Israel tells its story at the Passover meal, one of deliverance from slavery and entrance to the promised land (Exodus 12). This story is also told in the Passover Haggadah, that if the Lord had not brought our ancestors out of Egypt where they were slaves then we, our children, and our children's children would still be the slaves of Pharaoh. Jesus shares this Passover meal with his own disciples (John 13), and commands them to eat this meal in remembrance of him (Matthew 26, 1 Corinthians 11). Jesus feeds the multitudes (John 6), eats meals with sinners (Luke 15), and shares a mysterious meal with two of the disciples on the way to Emmaus (Luke 24). The first Christians break bread together and eat their meals with glad and generous hearts (Acts 2). Later, there are communal abuses of the practice of the Lord's Supper

(1 Corinthians 11).[1] One of the most misunderstood concepts in Christian faith and practice, the reference to eating the Lord's Supper in an unworthy manner referred to the experiences of gluttony and poverty at the common meal. The Christian hope was also shaped by the expectation of a Messiah who would preside over a great banquet (Luke 14). This core practice for the Christian community is rich in meaning and function. And yet, at a simple level, it is helpful for Methodists to know how this meal has shaped our own heritage.

FOR REFLECTION: CAN YOU DESCRIBE HOLY MOMENTS IN THE MEALS SHARED WITHIN YOUR CONGREGATION? CAN YOU IMAGINE THE LIFE OF THE CHURCH WITHOUT A FREQUENT CELEBRATION OF THE HOLY MEAL? WHAT WOULD HAPPEN TO THE QUALITY OF OUR RELATIONSHIP WITH GOD? CAN YOU RECALL HOLY MOMENTS IN YOUR OWN LIFE THAT OCCURRED OVER MEALS?

Hospitality

Family meals can take on different connotations; sometimes there is a special occasion, sometimes a sense of urgency, and at other times the meal is a common experience of nourishment and sustenance. As a Christian practice, receiving Holy Communion can also take on different meanings. On World Communion Sunday, we are conscious that we receive this grace with our brothers and sisters in Christ who worship throughout the world—in large urban cathedrals, in house churches, in the suburbs, in country parishes and in persecuted villages, in prison chapels and in nursing homes. On World Communion Sunday we remember those who are scattered throughout the earth, the one body who partake of the one bread, and our sense of space is enlarged. On All Saints Day, or on a Homecoming Sunday, we remember those men and women of faith who have gone before us. Our sense of time is enlarged in the Communion of Saints. These two days give us a glimpse of the richness of the feast. Observances in Lent, at Easter, and at Pentecost, and in ordinary time carry other connotations. World Communion Sunday and All Saints Day remind us that Jesus Christ and his grace are expansive, broad, and comprehensive. Charles Wesley's hymn text conveys this truth:

> O that the world might taste and see the riches of his grace!
> The arms of love that compass me would all the world embrace.[2]

And yet our practice is always at a particular moment in time, in a specific place in the world, in body of Christ, with a loaf of bread and a cup. The arms of God's love embrace the whole world, and each person is welcomed in the spirit of Charles Wesley's invitation: "Come, sinners, to the gospel feast!"[3] And that includes all of us!

As a basic practice, Holy Communion is a reminder that God provides grace for us. God is not limited in any way in his coming to us, but he has promised to meet us in this meal, to provide for us: "give us this day our daily bread." Jesus teaches us to pray. The phrase "daily bread" has multiple meanings. It can mean fresh bread, and those listening to Jesus would have been reminded of the gift of bread in the wilderness, manna, that was new every morning, and we remember that every time we sing another hymn:

> Great is thy faithfulness! Great is thy faithfulness!
> Morning by morning new mercies I see;
> all I have needed thy hand hath provided;
> great is thy faithfulness, Lord, unto me![4]

That hymn, pointing back to Jesus' teaching in John 6, that he is the bread of life (which itself pointed back to the Passover) is a reminder that God provides grace for us. "Great is thy faithfulness" and "Give us each day fresh bread," mean, I think, that we are praying for sufficient provisions for each day. None of us can truly secure the future, we cannot build fallout shelters that will protect us from biological terrorism or invest in stocks that will insulate us from economic shifts. We live one day at a time. And so we pray, give us this day *fresh bread,* a new experience of the truth that God provides grace for us. Great is thy faithfulness.

The meal is also a reminder that God's grace is available to all. John 6 is the account of the feeding of the 5,000, which all began with a boy who had five loaves and two fish. And the simple truth was that God's grace was not just for a few, not just for the disciples in the boat, but for all: "the arms of love that compass me would all the world embrace!"

Jesus made this point again and again in his teaching, and he modeled this truth in his life: God's grace is available to all. "He eats with sinners," some murmur under their breath in Luke 15, and so Jesus tells three of his great parables: a lost coin, a lost sheep, a lost son. The son of man has come to seek and save that which is lost (Luke 19:10). In *The Great Thanksgiving . . . for Baptism of the Lord or Covenant Reaffirmation,* we remember the life of our Lord in his way: "In his baptism and in table fellowship he took his place with sinners."[5]

In John Wesley's day, some felt they were unworthy to receive communion, and Wesley's response was that we are unworthy to receive any mercy from God, and yet that is the core of the gospel: "While we were yet sinners, Christ died for us" (Romans 5:8 KJV), while we were far off a banquet was prepared for us. Mortimer Arias, a former bishop of the Methodist Church in Bolivia, has commented on the relationship between these two practices, Holy Communion and evangelism:

> Surely the open table is much more than "eucharistic hospital-ity." It means open homes, open churches, and open communities. I sincerely believe that one of the most exciting frontiers of missionary outreach and evangelistic witness is through what I like to call "evangelization by hospitality."[6]

Arias is claiming the practice of the early Methodists: Come sinners to the gospel feast! God's grace is available to all. Some traditions believed that a person had to be converted before he or she could come to the table of the Lord. Wesley believed, after the example of the life of Jesus, that a man or woman could be converted by receiving the word of God through the elements of Holy Communion. "I am the bread that comes down from heaven and gives life to the world," Jesus said (John 6).

The meal is a reminder that the grace given to us now is a fore-taste of the banquet which is to come. One of the most reliable interpretations of the teaching of Jesus, "give us this day our daily bread," is that he is praying, give us this day our *bread for tomor-row.* This was an anticipation of the great banquet, where disciples would be gathered from the north and the south and the east and the west to sit at the table of the Lord. This is the great home-coming. Homecomings are not about the past, although we do remember. Homecomings are about the future. I recall a member of the first congregation I served, who took my wife and me under his wing and made his community our community. We shared many meals together at the seafood restaurant in this rural area, eating bread and fish. These were often times of commu-nion, confession, and thanksgiving. He has since passed to the other side, and I look forward to a homecoming with him, to the banquet, the great supper of the Lord.

In the liturgy we pray words that have past, present and future dimensions: "Christ has died, Christ has risen, Christ will come again."[7] *The United Methodist Hymnal* (1989) has a trinitarian structure (The Glory of God, The Grace of Jesus Christ, The Power of the Holy Spirit) that is grounded in the Community of Faith (church, Scripture, sacraments) and culminates in "A New Heaven and a New Earth." One of the moving hymns in the latter section is "Come Let Us Join Our Friends Above":

> Come, let us join our friends above who have obtained the
> prize,
> and on the eagle wings of love to joys celestial rise. [8]

Many of our friends have passed to the other side and have obtained the prize. And so we pray with Jesus: *Give us bread for tomorrow.* When we eat this bread and drink from this cup we claim the truth of another hymn: "Blessed assurance, Jesus is mine, O what a foretaste of glory divine."[9] The Christian practice of Holy Communion celebrates the *providence* of God, the *hospitality* of Jesus Christ, and the *foretaste* of his kingdom. As we come to the table, we know that God provides for us; that the grace of Jesus Christ is offered to all people, and that the meal we share here is an anticipation of the banquet that will bring together disciples from every kind of church, speaking every language with every accent, a banquet foreseen by Charles Wesley:

> Come, sinners, to the gospel feast,
> let every soul be Jesus' guest.
> Ye need not one be left behind,
> for God hath bid all humankind.[10]

Sacrifice

The United Methodist Church recently published a supplement to the *Hymnal* entitled *The Faith We Sing*. It includes praise choruses ("How Majestic Is Your Name"), gospel songs ("The Lily of the Valley"), and more recent contributions that have been used widely in various communities within the larger church ("I Was There to Hear Your Borning Cry," "Sing Alleluia to the Lord").

Included in this volume is a Charles Wesley text entitled "Victim Divine." This eucharistic hymn is based on Hebrews 10:12-22, and upon first listening it is unusual by our current standards: there is no repetition of text; there is within the hymn a complexity of design in the text's movement from beginning to end, a complexity that requires attention of the mind; and the hymn is multisensory (an attribute often given to contemporary or alternative worship). "Victim Divine" is also deeply scriptural, almost a commentary on the Hebrews text, and it is profoundly doctrinal, in that it wrestles with beliefs about God and Jesus Christ, the meaning of salvation, and authentic worship.

The first stanza is an affirmation of the grace of God in the sacrificial offering of Jesus Christ upon the altar. The sacrifice is "once offered up, a spotless Lamb." Here there is an echo of Hebrews 10:11-12 that describes the complete and sufficient offering of Christ, in contrast to that of the priests which are offered "again and again," and an echo of Exodus 12:5 that contains the instructions for the festival of the Passover ("Your lamb shall be without blemish"). Christ is the atonement for our sin and the Passover lamb that secures our salvation.

The second stanza places Christ in the "holiest place," the holy of holies, where the offering for sin and guilt is made. There he intercedes for us; the letter to the Hebrews holds together the *perfection* of Christ's sacrificial priesthood (7:26-27) and the *humanity* of his offering (4:14-15). In the holiest place, before God, Jesus prays for us, and the sprinkled blood, symbolic of mercy and forgiveness, extending back to the Passover and forward to the New Covenant "spreads salvation all around." Salvation is offered to all. Atonement is unlimited.[11]

The third stanza connects the offering of Christ with the events surrounding the crucifixion. "The smoke of thy atonement here darkened the sun and rent the veil." The darkness (Matthew 27:45; Luke 23:44) recalls the ninth plague (Exodus 10) and the prophetic vision of Amos:

> Why do you want the day of the Lord? It is darkness, not light.
> . . . On that day, says the Lord God, I will make the sun go down
> at noon, and darken the earth at broad daylight. (5:18, 8:9)

When Jesus cries with a loud voice and gives up his spirit (breathes his last breath), the offering is complete (Matthew 27:50). It is finished (John 19:30). At this moment, Matthew writes, "the curtain of the temple is torn in two, from top to bottom" (Matthew 27:51; Mark 15:38). Donald Juel likens the tearing of the temple in the death of Jesus to the opening of the heavens during Jesus' baptism (Matthew 3:16; Luke 3:21).[12] There is an openness to the Holy in the revelation (uncovering) of God who looks upon prodigal children as royalty.

This fourth stanza is marked by a multisensory character:

> He still respects thy sacrifice, its savor sweet doth always please;
> the offering smokes through earth and skies,
> diffusing life, and joy, and peace;
> to these thy lower courts it comes, and fills them with divine
> perfumes.

The burning of incense by the high priest was for the purpose of pleasing God. The sacrificial death of Christ (Ephesians 5:2) has cosmic dimensions, descending even to us.[13]

"Victim Divine" concludes with a remarkable statement about the meaning of salvation:

> We need not go up to heaven, to bring the long sought Savior
> down;
> thou art to all already given, thou dost e'en now thy banquet
> crown:
> To every faithful soul appear, and show thy real presence here!

Salvation is not our achievement or ascent to God. Salvation is God's gift to us, in the incarnation, in the One who empties himself and takes the form of a servant and becomes obedient unto death, even death on a cross (Philippians 2:7-8). God comes down to us, in the incarnate (human) Jesus, and in the material elements of Holy Communion. The real presence of Christ at the table, the body and the blood of the Lamb who takes away the sin of the world, has already been given to us. The sacrifice is complete, sufficient, and effective.[14] Therefore we enter the sanctuary with "a true heart in full assurance of faith" (Hebrews 10:22).

Communion texts, whether they be anthems or hymns, convey a variety of messages, among them *mystery*,[15] *invitation*,[16] *unity* ("One Bread, One Body"), and *spiritual hunger* ("You Satisfy the Hungry Heart"). "Victim Divine" recaptures the sacrificial meaning of Holy Communion, which lies at the heart of all other meanings, and places the experience of receiving the bread and the cup within both Old and New Testament traditions. Its depth is both challenge and gift, and yet it offers the potential for a human response to God that involves the whole self in all of the senses: singing the hymn, touching and eating the bread, smelling the incense, being in the midst of darkness, seeing a light which can no longer be covered. We do not need to go up to heaven to have a spiritual experience. In Christ, God has made that available to us here, now.

A Practice in Search of a People

Reflection on the practice (or neglect) of Holy Communion in mainline North America churches often takes the form of lament. For Methodists, this lament can be traced back to John Wesley and his sermon, "The Duty of Constant Communion" (1787). It is the duty of every Christian, Wesley argues, to take communion as often as possible. He then offers two reasons for this practice: God commands us to do this, and it is beneficial to us. The command is in the form of an instruction in how to observe a spiritual practice, and the benefit is likened to an ordinary human experience: "As our bodies are strengthened by bread and wine, so are our souls by these tokens of the body and blood of Christ."[17]

Even at the origins of Methodism, Wesley felt the need to engage in an argument with those who saw little essential value in the practice of Holy Communion. As heirs to this tradition, we do well to continue the argument with a culture that has marginalized this practice for a variety of reasons: we do not feel spiritual, or we know that we are imperfect (indeed Wesley responded to these very arguments). In a culture that hungers for the Spirit, we have not maintained the centrality of the table as source of life-giving food for the soul. In so doing we have loosened the bonds between the spiritual and the material, and we have allowed the spiritual life to become isolated from the Body of Christ that sustains it!

Of course, there are dimensions of this practice that present challenges to us: we recall the exclusion of Richard Allen and Absalom Jones from the fellowship of St. George's Church in Philadelphia. Allen, a freed slave and an active Methodist, would go on to found the African Methodist Episcopal Church in 1816 and serve as its first bishop. This experience indicates a lack of hospitality that has led to a continued division. In both respects the table of the Lord stands in judgment upon our failure to be hospitable and our willingness to settle for less than union with one another.

And yet the table is also a reminder of our human need for communion with God. Wesley's insight, that a person could be converted upon receiving communion, was one that displayed remarkable faith. His mother, Susanna, had reported the following experience:

> Two or three weeks ago, while my son Hall [Westley Hall, her son-in-law] was pronouncing those words, in delivering the cup to me, "The blood of our Lord Jesus Christ, which was given for thee," the words struck through my heart, and I knew God for Christ's sake had forgiven *me* all *my* sins.[18]

Holy Communion could be an experience of prevenient, justifying, and sanctifying grace, and for this reason its character has always been something of a mystery (note the Wesley hymn, "O Thou Who This Mysterious Bread," based upon the Emmaus passage in Luke 24:13-35; see chapter 1, "Searching the Scriptures").

As a gift of grace, Holy Communion calls forth our gratitude. The liturgy begins with the responsive greeting:

The Lord be with you.
And also with you.
Lift up your hearts.
We lift them up to the Lord.
Let us give thanks to the Lord our God.
It is right to give our thanks and praise.[19]

In Holy Communion we are really learning to practice the art of thanksgiving, which is a fundamental human need: to express gratitude to our Creator, with an offering that has come from the earth. And gratitude is expressed not only in individual devotion and corporate liturgy, but also in lives transformed by the liturgy. Ultimately, Holy Communion draws us closer to God and closer to one another. As the service concludes, we offer a prayer that:[20]

- "We may be for the world the body of Christ, redeemed by his blood"—this is our *mission on this earth.*
- God will "make us one with Christ, one with each other, and one in ministry to the all the world"—this is our *unity as a church.*
- "God will make us one, until Christ comes in final victory, and we feast at his heavenly banquet"—this is the *foretaste of the life to come.*

GRACE· ST. MATTHEWS - ST. PAUL'S - ZION

6. Life Together

FIRE IN WESLEY HOUSE —
SAMUEL PRAYED. BUT SUSANNA
GOT A LADDER!"

RENAME ALL U.M.C. AFTER
SAINTS, MARTYRS & FAITH MENTORS"

They committed themselves to the teachings of the apostles, the life together,
the common meal, and the prayers.

—Acts 2:42 (THE MESSAGE)

I shall endeavor to show that Christianity is essentially a social religion, and
that to turn it into a solitary religion is indeed to destroy it.

—John Wesley

The **local church** provides the most significant arena through which disciple-
making occurs. It is a community of true believers under the Lordship of
Christ. It is the redemptive fellowship in which the Word of God is preached by
persons divinely called and the sacraments are duly administered according to
Christ's own appointment. Under the discipline of the Holy Spirit, the church
exists for the maintenance of worship, the edification of believers, and the
redemption of the world.

—The Book of Discipline, 2000

One of my wife's favorite pastimes, especially if we are at the
beach or in the mountains, is to put together a big puzzle. At
times all of our family has gotten into the act. And you may share
this enthusiasm. I have another friend who takes it even more
seriously. He enjoys putting together the big, complex puzzles,
the ones that don't even have a picture of how it's going to end
up. You simply get started; you work on the corners and the
edges. Then you figure out the patterns, and a picture emerges.

That, it seems to me, is a good way to think about the church.
As we serve among God's people we get a picture. The pieces are
there, like a puzzle, but *we have to put it together!* And part of being

a pastor or a leader in the church is saying, "I'm going to help put the pieces of this puzzle together" or, "I'm going to be one of the pieces of this puzzle."

At Pentecost we are given a picture of how God's people live together. At the conclusion of Acts 2, there is an amazing portrait of a Christian community engaged in particular practices: they shared their possessions, they served those in need, they offered worship and praise to God, and they saw numerical growth within their fellowship. You might see the description of the early church in Acts 2:42 as a gathering of the essential pieces of this puzzle. They are the borders. They are how we get started in assembling a picture that makes sense.

The Teachings of the Apostles

Something remarkable had happened in the life and ministry of Jesus. And his followers were driven to talk about who he was and what he had done. They believed that Jesus of Nazareth was the Son of God, Lord, Savior, and that in his life, death, and resurrection, there was the hope of salvation. We also believe this. The apostles, like Peter and then Stephen and later Paul, would summarize their beliefs, and these became part of the New Testament. Other summaries were put together later: the Nicene Creed, in the fourth century, and the Apostles' Creed, in the sixth century.

These summaries focus on who Jesus is and who we are in relation to him. They are like a rule that keeps things straight. And without a rule, a summary, a specific body of content that has boundaries, there is no clarity of belief.

Part of the strength of the early Christian movement was that they had a clear sense of who they were and what had brought them together. "This Jesus whom you crucified," the formerly timid Peter announced with boldness, "God has made him both Lord and Messiah" (Acts 2:36).

Our picture must begin with the teaching of the apostles about who Jesus is and who we are in relation to him. Who is Jesus? This is the narrative that forms the Christian community, and the role of the leader in the community is to preserve the integrity of this narrative.[1] And yet there is always a tension between the past and the future, between the "story-formed community" (as articulated by Stanley Hauerwas) and our need for reformation. Thomas Langford defined this tension in the following way: "Doctrine reflects the grasp of the church; theology reflects the reach of the church. To use another analogy: doctrine is the part of the cathedral already completed, exploratory theology is creative architectural vision and preliminary drawings for possible new construction."[2] They committed themselves to the teachings of the apostles. There is another way to say this: it is not enough to feel or to do. We are also called to believe and to teach. This was the primary thrust of the pastoral epistles (1 and 2 Timothy and Titus) of the New Testament.

John Wesley took seriously the doctrinal formation of the early Methodist movement. He prescribed particular readings for preachers and leaders (indeed this was one of the primary reasons for the Annual Conferences). He summarized the doctrines of the faith passed to him and also responded to controversial topics of the day: note his famous essay "Predestination Calmly Considered." The United Methodist Church is guided especially by his example and by "Our Doctrinal Standards and General Rules," which are protected by Restrictive Rule 1 (¶ 16, *Book of Discipline*) and cannot be changed by the General Conference of the Church, which meets each four years. The Doctrinal Standards include the Articles of Religion of the Methodist Church and the Confession of Faith of the Evangelical United Brethren Church, as well as the Standard Sermons of John Wesley and his Explanatory Notes on the New Testament. Along with the Scriptures, these documents help create a picture—to employ Langford's analogy, perhaps a portrait of a cathedral. While it is a living cathedral, and there will be increased understanding of our heritage, we also recognize that all that is to be in the future will be built upon the foundation laid by those who have come before us.

The Life Together

Much of our time as pastors and church leaders is given to the ministry of conflict resolution. This is the result of our human sin. God's desire is that we all be one. While much attention is given to the visible signs of Pentecostalism in Acts 2, I am impressed with the aftereffects of Pentecost. When we know that God is one, and when we have begun to listen to each other, then we experience God's desire for us: *that we live in community*. The early disciples were committed to life together.

Life together is only possible when accountability and support are present. As with doctrine and theology, these exist in tension with each other. It is not accidental that one of the New Testament's ongoing questions was how to live a life of faithfulness in response to God's grace. Paul asks the question, "Should we continue in sin in order that grace may abound? . . . How can we who died to sin go on living in it?" (Romans 6:1, 2).

It is not accidental that the Doctrinal Standards collected in *The Book of Discipline* for United Methodists are closely followed, even connected, to The General Rules of The Methodist Church. Wesley's "Nature, Design, and General Rules of the United Societies" defines the vision of a life together: "A company . . . having the *form* and seeking the *power* of godliness, united in order to pray together, to receive the word of exhortation, and to watch over one another in love, that they may help each other to work out their salvation."[3]

This vision of life together was profoundly rooted in the New Testament: pray at all times in the Spirit (Ephesians 6:18); "exhort one another every day" (Hebrews 3:13); "tend the flock of God that is in your charge" (1 Peter 5:2); "work out your own salvation with fear and trembling" (Philippians 2:12). It incorporates *accountability* (watch over one another, receive the word of exhortation) and *support* (pray together, help one other).

Communities flounder when accountability and support are not held in tension. Without accountability, there is no discipline. But without support, there is no motivation or encouragement to progress in the Christian life.

This had been John Wesley's own experience, as the son of a mother who had high spiritual standards for her children and as a young adult participant in the Holy Club at Oxford. He understood that a grace-filled life could only be lived in a covenant community with others. His genius in establishing the Methodist movement was in combining a gospel of grace with an expectation that recipients of grace would meet together in groups.

John Wesley's vision for life together in these groups included General Rules that can be summarized in three categories:[4]

• Doing no harm
• Doing good
• Attending upon all the ordinances of God

While a reading of these rules might appear legalistic to our modern minds, they were in practice an experience of the organic nature of the early church, and they present for us a model to be reclaimed.

Two rediscoveries can be noted here. First, the substantive work of David Lowes Watson in defining covenant discipleship as "mutual accountability in acts of Christian discipleship" should be noted. Watson has translated Wesley's *General Rules* into "a new 'General Rule of Discipleship,' " that includes "works of mercy" (acts of compassion, acts of justice) and "works of piety" (acts of devotion, acts of worship).[5]

Second, the story of Christ Church United Methodist in Fort Lauderdale, Florida, a congregation that has experienced renewal through Wesley Fellowship Groups should be noted. Dick Wills, the pastor, was inspired to form these groups after a visit with Methodists in South Africa. He specifically refers to Acts 2:42-47 and to the Wesleyan model of United Societies, Class Meetings and Bands. These groups are instrumental in helping the congregation to fulfill its mission "to introduce people to Jesus in positive ways, to disciple believers through Wesley Fellowship Groups, and to relieve suffering."[6] And of course, our rediscovery of the importance of small groups occurs within a larger global experience, particularly the cell church movement, or megachurch movement, reunion groups that follow Cursillo and "Walk to Emmaus" retreats, recovery groups, and the base communities *(communidads de base)* of the Latin American church.

The Common Meal

In the ancient world, eating together was the way barriers were broken down. Notice in the Gospels how often Jesus shared meals with people of all kinds. Will Willimon reminds us that "eating together is a mark of unity, solidarity, and deep friendship."[7] Two things were evident in the common meal: God was bringing people together, and God's presence was in our midst.

For years my wife and I have had a habit of eating breakfast together in the mornings. In the evenings we are often going in different directions; we have more control over our mornings. I am quite sure that these meals are probably the glue that holds our relationship together.

It was true for the first disciples of Jesus. They shared the common meal together, a blending of communion and a congregational dinner. They would not have made a distinction between the two. We have reflected on the centrality of the common meal in our discussion of Holy Communion. Here it is important to remember the crucial relationship between life together and the sharing of meals.

The Prayers

The early Christians were a community of people who prayed for each other, in temple worship and in their homes. The early Christians were committed to the prayers. It happens even now. We pray with a family, in a circle, hands joined, when someone has died, or a youth mission team returns home safely, or someone goes into surgery. Prayer partners stay in touch over the Internet. Men gather early in the morning to pray. We pray for missionaries across the planet. Individuals use the *Upper Room* devotional, either in magazine or e-mail form, as a guide to personal devotion.

Prayer is an essential practice for the Christian. Wesley listed private and corporate prayers as ordinances of God and as means of grace. Prayer infuses all of the practices. As John Wesley wrote in a commentary on 1 Thessalonians 5:16 ("Pray without ceasing"): "Prayer may be said to be the breath of our spiritual life."[8] Craig Dykstra and Dorothy Bass have defined prayer in relation to practice in this way:

> Every Christian practice requires prayer, as Christians doing things together attune themselves to take part, with trust, in the risky activities of God. In prayer, we open ourselves to respond to God's presence and notice the light of God as it

shines on the world, exposing the fault yet also promising hope. We pay attention in a special way, focusing our yearning to be partners in God's reconciling love. We ask for God's help in saying yes to that which is life-giving in the deepest sense and in saying the specific no that will loosen whatever chains bind us and others to destruction. We thank God for life and love, and we beg God for mercy and strength, for ourselves and all creation.[9]

The emphasis here is upon prayer as a practice that Christians engage in together. The theologian Paul Jones has suggested that the Wesleyan form of Christianity can best be understood as corporate spiritual direction.[10]

Life Together as Christian Conferencing

The teaching of the apostles, the life together, the common meal, the prayers—when these are firmly in place, the picture begins to emerge. But it is not finished. There are other pieces to place in there. God will frame the borders of the picture, but you and I have to complete it. How will we do that? We seek spiritual guidance from each other. Christian conferencing was, for Wesley, an instituted means of grace (with conferencing being defined as consultation or advice). We listen. We pray. We confess. We watch over one another in love. And we recognize the uniqueness of each human being.

For this very reason United Methodist congregations, and the small groups within them, can look very different. There is a diversity of gifts (1 Corinthians 12); we live in different contexts; leadership is practiced in different ways. And yet Christian conferencing, sharing life together, holding accountability and support in tension, is an essential element in the practice of faith for United Methodists.

The miracle of Pentecost was an emerging Christian community. The miracle of early Methodism was an emerging Christian community. In the miracle, today happens when new faith communities are formed: congregations, classes, sharing groups, mission teams. A puzzle, any puzzle, requires every piece to be complete. And the miracle we await in our time is the recovery of Christian community, Christian conferencing, within United

Methodism. The picture of the church that God wants us to be will not be complete without the four important pieces I have described: the teaching of the apostles, the life together, the breaking of bread, the prayers. The hymn says it well: "I am the church! You are the church! We are the church together!"[11]

PART TWO

Implications

7. A Way of Life in the World: Spiritual Practice and the Recovery of Human Nature

I am the way, and the truth, and the life. No one comes to the Father except through me.

—John 14:6

Thou hast formed us for Thyself, and our hearts are restless till they find rest in Thee.

—Augustine

The origin of doctrine and its goal is the practice of the Christian faith.

—Scott J. Jones

Wesley's writing about the *imago Dei* (image of God), which is his primary way of describing the process of salvation in our lives, shapes my understanding of human nature as a pastor in The United Methodist Church. A contemporary theologian in the Wesleyan tradition, Geoffrey Wainwright, speaks of our similarity to God by employing the concept of the *imago Dei*, when speaking about our capacity to commune with God. This is our "original orientation."[1] Thus two of Wainwright's favorite theological statements are taken from the first Westminster Confession, the Presbyterian confession of faith: "What is the chief end of man? Man's chief end is to glorify God and to enjoy Him forever." The second is taken from Saint Augustine: "Thou hast formed us for Thyself, and our hearts are restless till they find rest in Thee."[2]

We are made for God, and we do not fulfill our humanity apart from the experience of divine presence. We are drawn toward God primarily through God's activity (revelation), yet we resist God. We are apt to ignore our vocation (communion with God, growth in the image of God) precisely because our love becomes self-love; we turn from the worship of God to self-idolatry, or *homo incurvatus in se*.[3] As in Romans 1, we exchange the truth of God for a lie; we ignore reality, which is, as Wainwright states, "towards God." Thus the image of God is distorted. Wainwright's emphasis on humanity understood as the image of God whose vocation is communion with God, does not imply that he has an exalted view of human nature. The relationship, as it is maintained between God and persons, is understood as divine gift, due to "the character of God, his intention for humanity, his action to achieve his purpose."[4]

Any pastor will immediately recognize this paradox—that we are drawn to God, and yet we also resist God—in her congregation and indeed within herself. The image of God within us communicates our capacity for God; the reality of sin is the barrier we construct to keep God at a distance. This internal struggle is at the heart of a Wesleyan understanding of human nature. Thus Albert Outler writes:

> The critical nuance here is the difference in [Wesley's] doctrine of "original sin" and "total depravity" from what Gilbert Rowe taught me to call "*tee*-total depravity" (i.e., the Lutheran and Catholic diagnoses of the human condition). The twofold clue here is in (1) Wesley's (essentially catholic) view of sin as a malignant *disease* rather than an obliteration of the *imago Dei* in fallen human nature, and (2) in his displacement of the doctrine of "election" with the notion of "prevenient grace."[5]

The presence of the *imago Dei* in some form in the human person allows the individual to move toward God, and indeed the movement is an act of (prevenient) grace. The movement is also the motivation for participation in Christian practices. Peter Böhler gave Wesley advice about the possibility of our participation in the means of grace *prior* to faith: "Preach faith til you have it, and then because you have it, you will preach faith."[6]

Sometimes discipline is prior to doctrine: our lifestyle leads into a new way of believing! And in his journal Wesley insists that, "The Lord's supper was ordained by God to be a means of . . . preventing, or justifying, or sanctifying grace. . . . No fitness is required at the time of communicating, but a sense of our state, of our utter sinfulness and helplessness."[7] The process of participation in Christian practices as a means of restoration of the image of God is also captured in the Charles Wesley hymn, "Love Divine, All Loves Excelling": "Take away our bent to sinning."[8] This process of the restoration of the image of God in us is what Wesley defined as sanctification. Thomas A. Langford's commentary is helpful:

> The experience of sanctification is the restoring of the defaced image of our creation. As fallen, persons have forfeited their authentic humanity; as sanctified, they are restored to and mature in the life that God intends. Human life is graced and reaches its goal of true joy. Wesley was aware that new birth into Christ can degenerate into *sentimental emotionalism, ineffective religiosity, or irrelevant piety*. The new person still lives in the flesh and in the world, so *the necessary corollary to liberation is discipline*; the sanctified life is shaped by God's demands and human faithfulness.[9]

The Way that Leads to Life: Shaped by Human Faithfulness

The sanctified life, the process of human nature restored into the image of God, is shaped by doctrine and discipline, what Wesley called "practical divinity." In Wesley's theology, the priority of grace was also closely followed by the necessity of the "means of grace." Wesley's movement was ignited by a revival that brought many into an experience of God's grace, but also produced additional problems. Albert Outler notes that the novelty of the revival was beginning to decrease, and it came to be surrounded by both persecution and misinterpretation. The first Annual Conference in June 1744 gathered together the "traveling preachers" of England and a few others to reflect on three questions:

- What to teach? (doctrine)
- How to teach?
- What to do? (discipline, practices)

In the second Annual Conference, August 1745, the following minutes are preserved:

> Q: 10. In what manner should we preach entire sanctification?
> A: Scarce at all to those who are not pressing forward; to those who are, always by way of promise, always drawing rather than driving.
> Q: 11. How then should we wait for the fulfilling of this promise?
> A: In universal obedience, in keeping all the commandments, in denying ourselves and taking up our cross daily. These are the general means which God hath ordained for our receiving his sanctifying grace. The particular [means] are prayer, searching the Scripture, communicating and fasting.[10]

In his sermon, "The Means of Grace," Wesley acknowledges the potential abuse of the forms of religion: "some began to mistake the *means* for the *end,* and to place religion rather in doing those outward works than in a heart renewed after the image of God."[11] But later he insists that the opposite extreme has become a reality. Many have come to despise or discount the ordinances; he continues:

> Yet it is not strange, if some of these, being strongly convinced of that horrid profanation of the ordinances of God which had spread itself over the whole church, and wellnigh driven true religion out of the world, in their fervent zeal for the glory of God and the recovery of souls from that fatal delusion, spake as if outward religion were *absolutely nothing,* as if it had *no* place in the religion of Christ. It is not surprising at all if they should not always have expressed themselves with sufficient caution; so that unwary hearers might believe they condemned all outward means as altogether unprofitable, and not designed of God to be the ordinary channels of conveying his grace into the souls of men.[12]

Wesley alludes to yet another perspective on the means of grace: those who have enthusiastically received the gospel, who "are usually impatient of their present state, and, trying every way to escape from it. They are always ready to catch at any new thing, any new proposal of ease or happiness. They have probably tried most outward means, and found no ease in them."[13] The modern equivalent is found in the person who says, "I am spiritual but I am not religious!"

My hunch is that most pastors and church leaders have encountered each of these persons referenced by Wesley in their congregations. There are those who are immersed in the activities and programs, the structure and organization of the church, with little interest in the spiritual life. There are others who sense that the Christian life must always be extraordinary and spontaneous; and there are others who chase one religious fad after another, but with little depth of habit. This comes near to Thomas A. Langford's earlier judgment of Christian experience as "sentimental emotionalism, ineffective religiosity, or irrelevant piety."

Yet for Wesley salvation was a process by which men and women came to a deeper and more profound understanding and experience of grace, and surely we have known persons in our congregations who would come to mind as being on this journey that Eugene Peterson has wonderfully named as "a long obedience in the same direction." Wesley would have said that they were partakers of the means of grace, which he defined as follows: "By 'means of grace,' I understand outward signs, words, or actions ordained of God, and appointed for this end—to be the *ordinary* channels whereby he might convey to men preventing, justifying, or sanctifying grace."[14] These he defined in the sermon as *prayer*, individual and corporate; *searching the Scriptures*; and receiving the *Lord's Supper*. He rejected the idea that these means could be understood as "seeking salvation by works." The theologian Serene Jones provides a helpful commentary in reminding us that the doctrine of justification by faith frees us from a "bondage of practices."[15]

Instead, these means were, for Wesley, "my waiting in the way God has ordained, and expecting that he will meet me there because he has promised so to do."[16] These means of grace have anthropological implications. In prayer we commune with God; indeed this is a primary dimension of what it means to be created in God's image.[17] In the reading of Scripture we are encountered by the Word of God that is both human and divine. In receiving the Lord's Supper we acknowledge the material creation (bread, wine) as blessed by God, and, as a sacrament, as an "outward and visible sign of an inward and spiritual grace." And the means of grace also shapes us ecclesiologically: as Craig Dykstra has noted, "Communities do not just engage in practices; in a sense, they *are* practices."[18]

Christian Practices, Means of Grace, and Restoration in God's Image

It is clear in Wesley's early writings that there were specific practices, or means of grace, that were suggested, or even required for the people called Methodists. It is also evident that congregations often have particular traditions related to these practices: ways of praying for one another and the world, and methods for finding resources for individuals in their prayer life; opportunities to hear the Scriptures and to study in worship and class settings; and services of Holy Communion.

I have begun to sketch the link between human nature, in the light of God's grace, and the means of grace, or practices that are the ordinary channels whereby God graces human life. A clearer definition of what I mean by practices has been offered by Craig Dykstra and Dorothy C. Bass as "things Christian people do together over time in response to and in the light of God's active presence for the life of the world."[19] I believe that congregations (and the people who compose them) are shaped by Christian practices. I am also aware that we do some things more as routine activities. For example, we might at times do things in routine ways without understanding the historical basis for doing them. A Christian practice, like celebrating Holy Communion or a service of healing or singing a hymn, can be rooted in sustained reflection on Scripture and tradition.

We can also do things in routine ways that are shaped more by the culture than by the Christian tradition, more by the patterns of a secular environment than by the faith. For example, the social life of a Christian may be more influenced by an "achievement-oriented lifestyle" and by self-securing than by practices such as hospitality, even though the external behaviors may appear to be very similar. Wesley would describe this as having the outward form without the appropriate inward disposition. In preparing the standard doctrines for the early Methodist churches in the years 1740–1760, Wesley left his *Explanatory Notes on the New Testament* and a collection of *Forty-Four Sermons*. Of these forty-four sermons, thirteen are taken from the Sermon on the Mount (Matthew 5–7), and a recurring theme in these sermons is the importance of what Wesley calls the "inward righteousness" in relation to external works.

Clearly our individual lives and our corporate mission can be divorced from God's grace. This can happen as we engage in routine ways in the business or busyness of the church, having the form but not the power of a godly life. This seems to have been the early experience of John and Charles Wesley.

A life of wholeness is defined by the integrity of doctrine and discipline, inward righteousness and external works. This was the genius of the Wesley's contribution to Christianity: linking heartfelt prayer with passionate outreach, individual piety with sacramental conviction, significant accountability with amazing grace. The way that leads to life is found in the wholeness that includes these facets of the Christian faith. And this wholeness, toward which we journey, is nothing less than the recovery of the image of God—our original orientation—within and among us.

8. The Experience of Christ: Lives Ordered by Grace

*For by grace you have been saved through faith, and this is not your own
doing; it is the gift of God—not the result of works, so that no one may boast.*

—Ephesians 2:8-9

Grace is the source, faith the condition, of salvation.

—John Wesley

In the midst of faults and failures, stand by me.
When I've done the best I can, and my friends misunderstand,
thou who knowest all about me, stand by me.

—Charles Albert Tindley, "Stand By Me"

Something Is Loose in the World (Prevenient Grace)

There was a small congregation in rural Georgia that was often
visited by a stray dog the children loved. Tom Long, who would
grow up to be one of the greatest preachers in the English language, according to one survey, was in that small congregation as
a child. He realized, later, "what a trial it must have been for our
ministers to attempt to lead worship and to preach on those
Sundays when this mongrel was scampering around the building
and nuzzling the feet of the congregation. . . . A dog loose in worship unmasks all pretense and undermines false dignity." [1]

I want to submit to you that this is not a bad way of beginning to think about how God is at work in our lives. For John Wesley, our ancestor in the faith, the core of the matter, the marrow, was salvation, and salvation was a process—something God does mysteriously over a span of time. The longer he lived, the more firmly he believed this. And for John Wesley, who read deeply from the Scriptures, salvation was all about the movement of grace in our lives.

Grace has been simply defined as something we do not earn, something we do not deserve, and something we cannot repay. Grace is at the heart of the New Testament—Jesus, hanging on the cross between two thieves—"Father, forgive them" (Luke 23:34); Paul, reflecting on the cross, and what happened at the cross, "God proves his love for us in that while we still were sinners Christ died for us" (Romans 5:8). *Were you there when they crucified my Lord?* We were all there, hanging on crosses, and Jesus is there between us, speaking to God on our behalf, "Father, forgive them." Jesus hanging on a cross, for you and for me, for the world, a reminder: *Something is loose in the world*. Grace.

There really is *another* way to think about salvation, and that is to think that we can save ourselves: that we can save ourselves by doing good works, that we can save ourselves by believing the right things.

But the apostle Paul and John Wesley had been down this road. If anyone could save himself or herself by doing the right things, Paul said, it would have been me, a Pharisee of Pharisees (Philippians 3). John Wesley was "methodical" in his religious life, he even came to the New World to convert the Indians, but he failed. Good works were not enough. Paul was a rabbi, and John Wesley was a scholar at Oxford. Knowing the right things was not enough. Salvation is not about doing the right things. Salvation is not about believing the right things. Salvation is about *grace*.

John Wesley believed that the grace of God was at work in our lives *before we were aware of it*. He called this *prevenient grace*, the grace that goes before our response! The prophet Isaiah cried out, "Listen to me, . . . The LORD called me before I was born, while I was in my mother's womb he named me" (Isaiah 49:1).

God searches for us, like a lost coin, like a lost son, like a lost sheep. God pursues us: "Surely goodness and mercy shall follow me all the days of my life" (Psalm 23:6). The grace of God is always there first. It is a gift, something that we do not earn, something that we do not deserve, and something that we cannot repay.

This story came to me on a retreat a few years ago, and was shared by a Lutheran pastor from Pennsylvania who had migrated to North Carolina. One morning he arranged to have breakfast with a friend. They arrived at the diner; they were seated in a booth, and were met by a waitress. My friend ordered two eggs over easy, a side of bacon, whole-wheat toast, and coffee.

The two friends talked and drank coffee, and soon the breakfast arrived. My friend noticed the eggs, the bacon, and the toast. But something else was on the plate: a light-colored grainy substance.

"What is this?" he asked the waitress, pointing to it. "Those are grits," she responded. "I didn't order them," he continued. "That's okay," she said, "you don't have to order them, they come with it." My friend was a little frustrated. "But I don't want to pay for them." "You don't have to pay for them—they're *free!*" And finally, my pastor friend just couldn't stop. "I'm still not going to eat them." And the waitress said, with firmness, "You can eat them, or you can leave them, that's your choice. Just consider them a gift!"

Grace is the *unmerited, free gift of God that is sufficient for all of our needs.* Sometimes we do not ask for the gift (like the grits). And sometimes we are not ready to receive the gift. Yet here is the point. It is God's nature to offer grace to us, grace that comes to us *before* we are ready to receive it. There is a wonderful hymn text:

> I sought the Lord, and afterward I knew
> he moved my soul to seek him, seeking me.
> It was not I that found, O Savior true;
> no, I was found of thee.[2]

We do not find God. God finds us. And that is grace. John Wesley used the term *prevenient grace* in contrast to another common Christian doctrine, predestination. Predestination was the conviction that some are saved and some are not, and that God knows this beforehand. I grew up not far from what some called a hard-shell, primitive church. One of their core convictions was that God had predestined some to be saved and some to be damned. And so this church would not send out missionaries, for they would only bring in the unsaved. John Wesley felt that predestination cut the nerve of both discipleship and evangelism. If we are predestined to be saved, why should we live a Christian life? And if God already has a plan for who is saved and who is not, why should we bother sharing the gospel?

Instead, he began with grace. Grace is God's gift of salvation, available to all. Wesley knew that God's grace was not only present in the church, but also in the world; not only among those who sat in the family pews in the cathedrals of England, but also among the coal miners. Wesley began to take the gospel to them, field preaching, which was illegal for most parish priests. When church officials said to him, allegedly, "Father John, stay in your parish," his response was simple: "The world is my parish."

In other words, God's grace is at work in the lives of people who are outside the church. I believe that leads us to a fuller, richer understanding of salvation. Many of us can point to a time of decision or profession or first commitment, but many of us also know that God was doing something in our lives before that. In my own life I think of Sunday school teachers, my mother and my grandparents, a high school friend and his parents; I think of my home church, which gave me opportunities to come closer to Christ—not that I always did, but something was happening. I think of retreats, and neighborhood canvasses, and Bible studies. As a teenager I worked in grocery stores, putting up stock, running a cash register, cleaning and mopping the floors. I think of Christian men who worked in the grocery business, and how the store would feel different when they entered it. As a teenager I directed our youth choir as a volunteer, even though I knew very little about music; and I played guitar in the youth musicals, mostly because this was where the girls were and I thought it would impress them. It didn't work for me! But *something was loose in the world, in my world.* It was the grace of God.

We don't become Christians in the abstract, and it doesn't happen in its fullness all at once. It is a historically extended and socially embodied experience. It is like a journey, and we can look back and see the signs. A few years ago I was watching a program on public television. It was the story of a Hispanic father in New York City who had lost his adult son. The son was mildly retarded, and was unable to read or respond to the normal channels by which missing persons were found. The family was poor, and they had no pictures of their lost son. Finally the father came upon an idea. He had pictures of himself made, and he personally plastered them on every signpost in that part of the city. In the end the miracle happened: the son recognized his father, and knew that his father was seeking him, and there was a reunion.

When we know that God loves us this much, a change begins to occur in us. This is called *repentance*, the turning of our lives in the direction of home, toward God. "Thou hast formed us for Thyself," Augustine said, "and our hearts are restless till they find rest in Thee" (*Confessions*, 1.1). Jesus says, at the beginning of the gospel, "The kingdom has come," grace is loose in the world, "repent, and believe in the good news" (Mark 1: 15).

In the great work of grace, we can keep God at a distance. We can make the wrong choices and God will allow us to suffer the consequences. God makes room for our freedom, although it is a freedom that leads to slavery. Salvation, Wesley said, is the journey from the porch, to the door, to the house. The porch is where we are when something has begun to stir in us, a love that will not leave us alone, a grace that is loose in the world, a gift that we know we did not earn, that we do not deserve, that we cannot repay, a sign that God is seeking us. The porch is where we leave everything that has weighed us down, and we place it there, we give it up, we surrender all, we repent, we change. We are facing a door, and we are faced with a decision. Because, brothers and sisters, something is loose in the world. It is the grace of God.

A Door Opens (Justifying Grace)

One summer evening I was sitting in the stands at a minor league baseball game. It wasn't going very well for our team; it was hot, a little breeze here and there. A man was hawking ball caps and T-shirts. Occasionally someone would come by with a handful of beverages. The usual diversions—the kids running around the bases, the chicken dances, the off-key singing of "Take Me Out to the Ball Game," it was all happening. They announced the lucky ticket number. It wasn't mine. Then they asked the evening's medical question that a local hospital sponsors: "What material is inside the bone?"

That was the question: *what is the material that is inside the bone?* I didn't know the answer, but later in the game I found out: marrow. Marrow is the material that is inside the bone. John Wesley spoke of our beliefs about salvation as the marrow, the core, the essential thing. What do we believe about salvation? Is it important? Do we care?

John Wesley was concerned about the *marrow*, the core, of Christianity. And I want to talk about it in relation to what is *not* the core, what is external to it. The marrow, Wesley said, was *grace* and *faith* and *salvation*. Grace, according to Wesley, is the source of our salvation, and faith is the condition. We have discussed prevenient grace, the gift of God offered to us. Wesley likened this phase of the Christian life to the porch, all that leads up to faith, all that makes faith possible.

As we reflect on grace and faith and salvation, we are at the door. We are at the door because of grace. Grace is the working of God in our lives, a grace that puts us in a position to respond. Maybe our parents brought us to church. Maybe we experienced human love in such a way that we knew God's love might be real. Maybe we were forgiven for something, and there was a new beginning in our lives. Maybe we found a group of Christian friends in a Sunday school class or a Bible study or a choir or a circle or in our neighborhood, and we felt that we belonged. All of this is grace. Grace is the source of our salvation. Faith is the condition. The author of Hebrews defines faith in this way: "Faith is the assurance of things hoped for, the conviction of things not seen" (Hebrews 11:1).

I read a wonderful description of faith. A tightrope walker made his way across a deep gorge, balancing with a long pole. After accomplishing this feat, he asked the crowd, "Do you think I can do this again, this time pushing a wheelbarrow?" Some thought he could; others were skeptical. He walked successfully with a wheelbarrow, and everyone was thrilled. He then asked the audience, "Do you think I can do this again, this time pushing the wheelbarrow across with someone sitting in the wheelbarrow?"

By now the crowd had seen him do this twice, so they were enthusiastic in their support and belief that he could do it. He then asked, "Who would like to ride in the wheelbarrow?" At this point their enthusiasm turned to silence.[3] This story teaches us a great deal about faith, which really combines two realities: belief and trust. Belief is more than an awareness that somewhere God exists (Wesley pointed out that the Greeks and Romans knew this), and more even than the conviction that Jesus is Lord (Wesley pointed out that the devil knew this). We can know words, like the Apostles' Creed or the Lord's Prayer or even the words to a hymn or praise chorus, but that is not faith.

Belief must always be joined to trust. We may believe that the man can get across the deep gorge with the wheelbarrow, but it is another thing to trust ourselves to him, to place ourselves in his hands. That is belief *and* trust. And *belief plus trust equals faith*. It is important to know the Scriptures, for they point us to Christ. Believing in the right things is important. But it is also essential that we move from a mental assent—belief—to what Wesley called a "disposition of the heart."[4]

Trust is truly the marrow, the core of life. Many of us have had difficult experiences in life and we are wary of trusting people. A Gallup poll recently reported that trust in institutional religion is at its lowest point in 30 years. The church ranked sixth, behind the military, the police, the presidency, the U.S. Supreme Court, and banks. The church's betrayal of some of its members, so much in the media this past year, is one example of why trust is so difficult. A prominent newspaper columnist, a governor of one of our states, a congressman, an athlete—betrayal of trust is also there in the wider culture. Within families, within circles of friends, it is closer to home and more devastating. A betrayal, a dishonesty—people are not inclined to trust, and it is almost understandable.

The church is at its best when it does not call people to trust in it, as an institution, but in the One who calls us together as his Body, Jesus Christ. The church is the external matter that is outside the marrow. The church is not the core. The core is the faith that has been passed down to us. "The church's one foundation," we sing, is "Jesus Christ her Lord."

Faith (belief and trust, joined together) is the *condition* of salvation: by grace—the source—you have been saved through *faith*,

Paul writes. What then does salvation mean? It may not be the burning question we wrestle with each day, but even if you haven't thought about it in a while, it is the marrow, it is the core, and it is the essential. As Stephen R. Covey, a businessman, has remarked, "The main thing is to keep the main thing the main thing." Wesley answered the question—of what salvation means by reflecting first on what salvation is not. Salvation is not something that happens in the future, it is not the soul going to paradise, it is not the life to come. Note the words of Paul: "By grace you have been saved," not you *will* be saved. It *is* the gift of God, not it *will be* the gift of God.

Salvation is a *present* reality. It is, more precisely, the forgiveness of sins. It is an assurance that this God whom we have heard about is real. John Wesley was the son of an Anglican priest, a dedicated student and a zealous believer, so much so that he left England for a time to be a missionary. This experience was not positive; he had failed, and was more or less driven back home. On the way he traveled by ship with a group of Moravians, and they seemed to have an inner peace that he lacked. Wesley was utterly confused. He was a preacher, and he asked Peter Böhler, one of the Moravians, "How can I preach if I do not have faith?" Böhler responded, "Preach faith till you have it, and then because you have it, you will preach faith." He returned to London, to his home. He began to read the New Testament with new eyes. He fasted. He took Holy Communion as often as possible. He went to a church service at Saint Paul's Cathedral in London. The anthem was based on Psalm 130: "Out of the depths have I cried unto thee, O LORD" (KJV).

Even though he lacked faith, he participated in church. He was in the right places, near the source of salvation, which was grace. In his journal of May 24, 1738 he described the moment in his life where belief and trust came together:

> In the evening, I went very unwillingly to a society in Aldersgate Street, where one was reading Luther's Preface to the Epistle to the Romans. About a quarter before nine, while he was describing the change which God works in the heart through faith in Christ, I felt my heart strangely warmed. I felt I did trust in Christ, Christ alone for salvation; and an assurance

was given me that he had taken away *my* sins, even *mine*, and saved *me* from the law of sin and death.[5]

Note the key words in his experience: "the *change* which God works in the *heart* through *faith*. . . . I did *trust* in Christ, *Christ alone* for my salvation. . . . an *assurance* was given me that he had taken away my sins, even mine, and *saved me."*

The book of Acts tells the story of the first Christian martyr, Stephen. As he is being stoned to death, he says, at the end of chapter 7, of those who are killing him, "Lord, do not hold this sin against them." It is an echo of Jesus' words on the cross in Luke 23: "Father, forgive them." Saul, who would later be given a new name, Paul, is there. Luke, who wrote the book of Acts, writes that Saul approved of their killing Stephen.

Many believe that this was the beginning of the unraveling of Paul's religious life, from a salvation through his own righteousness to something else. On the way to Damascus he is struck blind. The Lord speaks to him. He receives the Holy Spirit, his eyes are opened, he is baptized. It is the amazing grace of God. Throughout the world, before synagogues and kings and pagans and philosophers, Paul tells the story of his experience. He has passed from darkness to light. His sins have been forgiven through the death and resurrection of Jesus Christ. And so he can write to the church at Ephesus: You were dead, we were dead in our sins, in our way of life that was contrary to God. But God is rich in mercy. "By grace you have been saved through faith. This is not your own doing" (Ephesians 2:8).

The heart of faith is not what *we* do or say. It is the One who carries us across. It is the One who stands by us. "It is a gift of God, not the result of works, so that no one may boast." This is a reminder to those of us who have been Christians for some time. It is not an achievement. It is not an accomplishment. Salvation is something different. It is *pure gift*. It comes to us from beyond ourselves. And the condition for our receiving it, saying yes to it, opening the gift, sitting in the wheelbarrow, is faith. Salvation is not only grace. It is also faith. Grace plus faith equals salvation.

Faith is opening the door. John Wesley believed that for some faith was instantaneous, a specific moment in time, when we gave our lives to Christ. For others, faith was gradual, it happened over weeks, or months, or years. In the New Testament there is Paul, who has a particular moment in time, and Timothy, whose faith comes more gradually, from one generation to another and to another.

God sets before us an open door. If you have opened the door, please know that this is not where it ends. There is more to the Christian life than accepting Jesus as your Lord and Savior. Someone has said that accepting Christ is like the kickoff—you can't have a game without it, but there are still four quarters to play. We need to talk about the true purpose of the Christian life, what happens after we step onto the porch and open the door, what it means to live in the house.

Why New Birth Is Not Enough (Sanctifying Grace)

We have reflected on the grace of God that goes before our response, of the action of God on our behalf that precedes any decision that we make. "You did not choose me," Jesus says in the Gospels, "but I chose you." This is the *prevenient* grace of God, and we see it, this morning, as a baby is baptized. We have examined our own response to God's gift. "By grace you have been saved through faith," Paul wrote to the Ephesians (2:8). We have considered the core beliefs of Methodists, John Wesley's wrestling with God's gift of amazing grace. Wesley favored "plain speech," and one of his best pictures was a simple one:

- Prevenient grace and repentance—all that happens prior to our response—is the *porch* of religion.
- Justification by faith—our acceptance, our yes—is the *door* of religion.
- And Holiness, or Sanctifying Grace is the *house* of religion. It is everything we do after we say Jesus Christ is Lord.

We have talked about being on the porch and opening the door. Now we reflect on what it means to live in the house, the fulfillment of our true purpose as God's people.

When someone becomes a Christian, it's like a new birth. To shift the metaphor, we noted that acceptance of Christ is like a kickoff at a football game. You can't have a game without it, but there are still four quarters left. Or, to change the picture again, as one of my favorite hymns, written by a contemporary Methodist pastor, announces, "Let every instrument be tuned for praise!"[6] And so we ask after becoming a Christian:

- What happens after our new birth?
- What happens in those four quarters after the kickoff?
- What happens after the instruments are tuned for praise?

We have crossed the porch. We have opened the door. What happens next? I had a wonderful friendship with a man who was a farmer, and whenever I would go out to see him, he would greet us with a deep laugh, "Come in the house!" That's what God is saying to us: "Come in the house!"

When we experience new birth, a wonderful adventure begins. But it is a tragedy if we never move beyond the experience of new birth. Births are always occasions for celebration. But a part of our celebration is the hope, the expectation that the child will grow up, mature, learn to walk, leave home.

You know the parable of the prodigal son. It is found in the fifteenth chapter of Luke. The son goes away, hits bottom, and wastes his inheritance. Then he comes to himself, and returns home. The son says, "I'm back." The father rejoices, "My son was dead and is alive, was lost and is found!" They have a feast that lasts long into the night. Everyone is happy!

The next morning, the son sleeps in. Everyone else rises early. The work begins. The son goes around to everyone who is at work, and says to him or her, "I'm back." And they all respond, "Bless God, you're back." The next morning, the son sleeps in again, makes his rounds with everyone, "I'm back, I'm back." This goes on for a while, until the day comes when someone finally says, "Bless God, you're back, here is a shovel, get to work!"[7]

New birth is not enough. Paul, writing to the early Christians, let them know that by now he would have expected them to have moved beyond milk to solid food. Accepting Christ is like a new birth, but there is life after birth.

This life, according to Wesley, was called *holiness,* or *growth in grace,* or *sanctification.* This life was becoming a new creature, the image of God, disfigured by our sin, being restored in us. It is progress, maturity, discipleship. And yet it is a progress made possible by the prior action of God. A hymn by Charles Wesley, based upon Ephesians 2:8-10 and with an allusion to Galatians 5:6, expresses this well:

> Let us for this faith contend, sure salvation is the end;
> heaven already is begun, everlasting life is won.
> Only let us persevere till we see our Lord appear,
> never from the Rock remove, saved by faith which works by
> love. [8]

The great key to what it means, for Wesley, to progress in the Christian life is *love*. He defined holiness as love of God and love of neighbor. We don't love God because God is perfect, although he is. We love God because God first loved us. It is also not enough to have faith. "The only thing that counts," Paul wrote to the Galatians, "is faith working through love" (Galatians 5). "If I have faith powerful enough to move mountains, but have not love," Paul wrote, "I gain nothing" (1 Corinthians 13). The test of our faith is love.

Sometimes I will talk with couples prior to their weddings. I will ask a few questions, and I will listen to their responses. Sometimes I will ask, "Why do you love each other?" People can be really eloquent about that one, or they can stumble all over it! I will then point out that there is very little in a wedding service itself about romantic love. The wedding vows are promises. You've heard them: for better, for worse, for richer, for poorer, in sickness and in health. These promises are made in a moment when love is intense. But we almost anticipate that the day will come when the romance will subside, and like the hard truth of a country song, the feeling is gone.

In this way the promises will sustain the marriage. This is the love we read about in 1 Corinthians 13: "Love is patient; love is kind; love is not envious or boastful or arrogant or rude. It does not insist on its on way. . . . It bears all things, believes all things, hopes all things, endures all things. Love never ends."

"The only thing that counts," Paul wrote, "is faith working through love" (Galatians 5:6). This is the ultimate test of our belief, of our faith, of our maturity. *Does it produce the fruit of love?* When God says, "Come in the house!" it's all about love. When the scribe asks Jesus which is the greatest commandment, the Lord responds, "Love the Lord your God with all your heart, and with all your soul, and with all your mind, and with all your strength. . . . Love your neighbor as yourself." The scribe repeats these words back to Jesus, and the Lord responds again, "You are not far from the kingdom" (Mark 12:30-34). In other words, "you've got it."

John Wesley had some specific and concrete convictions about love:

- Love doesn't happen by accident. God uses ordinary channels to help us grow in grace: private and public prayer, reading the Scripture, listening to others teach it and preach it, and receiving Holy Communion as often as we can. He also believed in the accountability—gained by class meetings— where we are reminded of the promises we made before God.
- Love is both *internal* and *external*. We need to pay attention to the inside of the house and the outside of the house. We are called to love God and to love our neighbor. In fact, they are connected and inseparable. The inside of the house, fundamentally, is *gratitude*. The outside of the house is *benevolence*. We are put on the earth to love God and our neighbor. That was the core of Wesley's belief about sanctification. His mission was to call together a church that would help people do this in practical ways.
- Love is a work in progress. This image may help. Marianne Williamson said, you ask God into your life, your spiritual house, and you think he is going to find a few things need touching up. And you're thinking, "This is pretty good." Then one day there is a wrecking ball outside. You'll have to start over with a new foundation.[9] This is the difficult work of becoming a new creation. This is the difficult journey of holiness. This is the difficult part of accepting God's invitation. "Come in the house," God says. Something in us wants to accept the invitation, to live in the house. But some part of us wants to hang out on the porch for a while, because we are resistant to change.

FOR REFLECTION: DO YOU EVER FIND YOURSELF RESISTING CHANGE?

When C. S. Lewis was a child he knew that if he told his mother he had a toothache she would give him something for the pain for that night. But he did not always tell her, because he knew that his mother would give him not only an aspirin, but also that the next morning she would take him to the dentist. He remembered it this way: "I could not get what I wanted out of her without getting something more, which I did not want. I wanted immediate relief from pain: but I could not get it without having my teeth set permanently right."[10]

Once God begins the work of salvation in our lives, he is not content until we are remade into his image, which is love. God is love. Any understandings of salvation that settle for less than these deny the ultimate power of God's grace. We never find a resting place as Christians—we are always in the process of being saved, of becoming more like Jesus. And God is never finished with us. The early Methodists lived in the daily awareness of this profound hope. There is a new birth, but we will also learn to walk, and run and not be weary, we will even mount up with wings like eagles. The instruments can be tuned for praise, so that we can play the music that breathes from within us, for which we were created. The Wesleys were convinced, despite "fightings and fears within, without" and obstacles seen and unseen, that "the one who began a good work among you will bring it to completion" (hymn, "Just as I Am, Without One Plea," Philippians 1:6). On this Charles Wesley has the last word, a prayer offered in confidence and assurance:

> Finish, then, thy new creation; pure and spotless let us be.
> Let us see thy great salvation perfectly restored in thee;
> changed from glory into glory,
> till in heaven we take our place,
> till we cast our crowns before thee,
> lost in wonder, love, and praise.[11]

9. Rediscovery of Tradition as a Means of Grace

Rekindle the gift of God that is within you through the laying on of my hands; for God did not give us a spirit of cowardice, but rather a spirit of power and of love and of self-discipline.

—2 Timothy 1:6-7

To serve the present age, my calling to fulfill; O may it all my powers engage to do my Master's will!

—Charles Wesley

What I am, therefore, is in key part what I inherit, a specific past that is present to some degree in my present. I find myself part of a history and that is generally to say, whether I like it or not, whether I recognise it or not, one of the bearers of a tradition. . . . Practices always have histories and . . . at any given moment what a practice is depends on a mode of understanding it which has been transmitted often through many generations.

—Alasdair MacIntyre

Our older daughter, Liz, is a rock collector. She knows a great deal about all kinds of rocks and gems, and has a real love and fascination for them. One summer, on a family vacation, we had spent a couple of days in the mountains near Asheville and were on our way to my mother's house in Georgia. So we decided to cut through the very westernmost part of North Carolina and stop in Franklin, to spend some time in the gem mines.

It was a rainy day, muddy, messy, but there we were. We raced out of our cars, got underneath one of the sheds, and spoke to a gentleman about panning for gems. We were given several large bags of mud, and we began sifting and searching, exploring and prospecting, and along the way there was a nice piece here and a sparkle there, and "real find" here. Liz was elated, and as focused as I have ever seen her.

I remembered that experience in reflecting on the argument of this book—that renewal can come to the people called Methodists as we rediscover the riches of our heritage by putting them into practice. In one of the parables, Jesus likens the kingdom of God to the discovery of hidden treasure. But not hidden in some far-away, exotic place, like Nepal or Machu Picchu. It's not even hidden in the Holy of Holies, in the Temple, or in some other holy place. It's hidden in a field. The treasure is hidden in plain sight, right before us, but just beneath the surface.

To believe, to receive this gospel, is like finding treasure, it's like discovering grace. You may have heard the wonderful story about a rabbi who lived in great poverty, but whose faith in God was never shaken:

> Rabbi Eisik . . . dreamed someone bade him look for a treasure in Prague, under the bridge which leads to the king's palace. When the dream recurred a third time, Rabbi Eisik prepared for the journey and set out for Prague. But the bridge was guarded day and night and he did not dare to start digging. Nevertheless he went to the bridge every morning and kept walking around it until evening.
>
> Finally, the captain of the guards, who had been watching him, asked in a kindly way whether he was looking for something or waiting for somebody. Rabbi Eisik told him of the dream which had brought him here from a faraway country. The captain laughed: "And so to please the dream, you poor fellow wore out your shoes to come here! As for having faith in dreams, if I had had it, I should have had to get going when a dream once told me to go to Cracow and dig for treasure under the stove in the room of a Jew—Eisik, son of Yekel, that was his name! Eisik, son of Yekel! I can just imagine what it would be like, how I should have to try every house over there, where one half of the Jews are named Eisik, and the other Yekel!" And he laughed again. Rabbi Eisik bowed, traveled home, dug up the treasure from under the stove, and built the House of Prayer.[1]

In the Gospel, when the finder discovers the treasure, he's *ecstatic*. This is at the core of Christianity. Christianity is like finding treasure, it's like the discovery of grace. The treasure we are seeking is often found in the very fabric of our ordinary lives. The preacher Barbara Brown Taylor tells the following story:

> A poor single mother of three is notified of her maiden aunt's death in a distant city. Since she is the woman's only kin, she buys a bus ticket with the end of her grocery money and goes to sort through the old woman's things. Packing her aunt's old brown wool coat in a box for the Salvation Army, she feels something stiff down around the hem and discovers hundred dollar bills sewn into the lining.[2]

Sometimes we have to go to some lengths to discover grace. Sometimes we have to dig to discover grace: perhaps the discovery that a John Wesley was much more complex in his thinking than we might have realized. Sometimes we stumble over it and discover grace: in the verse of a Charles Wesley hymn, or in something that happens in our congregation that had almost seemed routine and now seems to be an open door to something richer. And sometimes we discover that grace is right in front of us. Christianity is like finding treasure; it's like the discovery of grace.

And there is a joy, an ecstasy in finding treasure, in discovering grace. And that joy, that ecstasy leads us on. This ecstasy is surely present in the words of Charles Wesley, "O for a thousand tongues to sing my great Redeemer's praise, the glories of my God and King, the triumphs of his grace!"[3]

When we find the treasure, when we discover the grace, we are compelled by a sense of urgency and sacrifice. There is urgency and sacrifice in both sayings of Jesus: "In his joy he goes and sells all that he has and buys that field. . . . On finding one pearl of great value, he went and sold all that he had and bought it" (Matthew 13:44-46).

When we find treasure, when we discover grace, something remarkable, but something we can all understand, happens here. In each case, when treasure is found, when grace is discovered, the finder makes a judgment: "The treasure I have found, the grace I have discovered, is of more value to me than anything else."

Do we believe that? Do we believe that the kingdom of God, the experience of salvation through the grace of Jesus Christ, is of more value than anything else? How we answer that question is at the heart of these parables. And how we answer that question has everything to do with what we are willing to give up in order to make that grace our own, that treasure a part of our lives.

In meditating on this parable I have not grasped the urgency of the gospel and the sacrifices I am called to make. I live and work in a culture that makes every possible commodity seem urgent— even the trivial—and that asks us to make sacrifices for things our children might be doing that are at best worthwhile and at worst the fad of the moment. There is an urgency about the gospel. When we have found treasure, when we have discovered grace, we will do whatever we have to do to make that a part of our lives. And that is *sacrifice*.

Two Invitations

There are two invitations at the conclusion of this book, an invitation to individuals and an invitation to the church. There may be some who have read thus far and have never experienced the grace of Jesus Christ. You have been trying to be good enough, pure enough, righteous enough, religious enough, and you have failed, and you're saying, "God, I'm not good enough," and God says, "I know." You're saying "God, I can't do this by myself," and God says, "You're beginning to understand." You're saying, "I give up," and God says, "Aha, you have found treasure, you have discovered grace."

To you the invitation is to *accept the grace of Jesus Christ in your life*. That may be your discovery. It is the greatest discovery you'll ever make. If this has been your discovery I urge you to become a part of a congregation that will connect you with the means of grace described in these pages:

- Searching the Scriptures
- Generosity with the poor
- Testimony
- Singing
- Holy Communion
- Life together

The connection between the grace of Jesus Christ and the means of grace (practices of faith) is essential. We cannot live the Christian life in individualistic or isolationist ways!

There is a second invitation, to the church. It is an invitation to respond to the claims of urgency and sacrifice in the gospel. My love for the Methodist tradition has led me to the conviction that we are at an important moment in our history. God has given us these wonderful practices, and yet we are in danger of losing them. The urgency is that they must be passed down from generation to generation—they are historically extended. And they are necessarily passed down from generation to generation by the church—they are socially embodied.

The pastors and leaders of our church must make the sacrifice. We must seek a rediscovery of these core practices that transcend the issues that have divided us. We must recognize that, at times, segments of the church that we call "liberal" have been more faithful in some of the practices, and at other times people that we label "conservative" have preserved some of the other practices. We must sacrifice, or relinquish, our preconceptions about our own strengths and the weaknesses of others. Woven together, these practices add up to a way of life that is truly a thing of beauty.

We are also at an important moment in American religious life, where, as a friend has noted, "everything is up for grabs" and "anything done well stands a chance of sticking." Many come into membership in United Methodist congregations looking for a particular spirituality, and they do not find it. They may be seeking a different treasure that is not a part of our tradition. I want to suggest that we point them toward the treasure that is a way of life, the culmination of many practices and activities that reinforce each other. We have something to offer American Christianity: the treasure of the gospel in our own earthen vessel.

We are sometimes faced with a more fundamental problem: if the gospel of grace, as it has been socially embodied and historically extended by the streams of Christianity that now compose The United Methodist Church has no urgency, if it is not sacrificial, then we have not found the treasure. Our task may be a reconsideration of the first invitation.

A final word—one of the most interesting interpretations of this parable goes like this: in the second parable, where the merchant goes in search of fine pearls, we tend to think that we are the merchant, looking for something. But what if God is the merchant who is seeking us, searching for us, finding us?[4] What if we are the pearl of great price? What if God would *urgently sacrifice* everything to find us, to claim us, to love us, to make us his own, and to use us? And what if this was the very truth expressed in the question of Charles Wesley: "O love divine, what hast thou done?"

Can you believe that God is as focused on locating us, as delighted in finding us as a young girl would be in discovering gems on a hot summer day in the mountains? Your life, my life, is the treasure God is seeking. God wants our treasure. Admittedly, it is a treasure that is contained in an earthen vessel. The treasure is graced human nature, the renewal of the image of God. For this Jesus was born among us—in the words of Charles Wesley's carol:

> Hark! the herald angels sing,
> "Glory to the newborn King;
> peace on earth, and mercy mild,
> God and sinners reconciled!"[5]

The reconciliation of God and sinner is made possible by grace. And a life of grace is sustained by the means of grace, the practices of our faith. If we are to live a sustainable faith, and if our tradition is to not only survive but also flourish, we will rediscover the treasure that is ours—these spiritual practices that convey the grace of God—as the people called Methodists.

Appendix One:
Resources for United Methodist Spiritual Practice

The listing of resources in the following pages is merely suggestive and not exhaustive. Core organizations within our church are not listed (United Methodist Women, United Methodist Men, United Methodist Youth). Institutions that have been at the heart of the Methodist presence in the world—educational institutions, health care ministries, urban and rural initiatives, Wesley Foundations—are wonderful examples of how Methodists have practiced their faith in the world. The Methodist movement is truly global in character; one thinks of the remarkable work being done in Eastern Europe, in Latin America, in South Africa, and again these merely hint at all that is taking place. Movements beyond our own tradition, such as Habitat for Humanity and Stephen Ministry have shaped and been shaped by Methodists who practice their faith within them. I encourage you to consider these resources in light of our discussion, and to make your own connections with them and with others that help you in the practice of faith.

The Spiritual Formation Bible

This version of the Scriptures was first published in 1999, and has included both the *New International Version* and the *Revised Standard Version* of the Bible. Apart from the biblical text, the *Spiritual Formation Bible* includes introductory statements and explanatory articles that lead the reader to approach the Scripture in a new and different way. Many of the writers and editors of these articles are associated with *The Upper Room* and *Weavings* magazines, publications affliated with the General Board of Discipleship of The United Methodist Church.

The particular articles include instruction on "praying the Scriptures," "*lectio divina*," and reading the Scripture formationally, in contrast to informationally. In this way the Scripture functions less like material to be mastered and more like a word from God addressed to the church and the individual. There are also individual reflections alongside the Scripture that come from Christian tradition. Augustine, John of the Cross, Martin Luther, Brother Lawrence, Julian of Norwich, John Wesley, and others are among those cited. In this way the *Spiritual Formation Bible* encompasses both Scripture and the living tradition that is a reflection on Scripture. For those who want to "search the Scriptures," the *Spiritual Formation Bible* is an excellent resource.

Disciple Bible Study

The United Methodist Publishing House launched the *Disciple Bible Study* in 1987 in response to a number of other highly intensive Bible studies that were present in congregations and communities. Written by Bishop Richard and Julia Wilke, *Disciple* is a 34-week study of approximately 80 percent of the Bible. Each week's class is designed as a two and a half-hour study, and the ideal group size is twelve persons and a leader. There are six days of readings and a Sabbath each week, with a suggested space for journaling responses to the assigned passages.

Disciple is unique in many respects. It includes a broad reading of a significant portion of Scripture, and yet it also focuses in depth each week on one particular passage. A trained leader guides the study, and yet students are given the freedom to respond as the Holy Spirit leads them. The individual reflection on Scripture is crucial, but is always tempered by the group's understanding. Mastery of historical, literary, social, and theological content is central to *Disciple*, but the movement of each session is always toward the question of "How is the Scripture calling me to be a disciple?"

One of *Disciple*'s strengths is that it is truly ecumenical, and thus is very much in the spirit of the Wesleys, who drew from a variety of traditions. The presenters are from the Jewish, Catholic, Protestant, and Evangelical traditions, and there is significant racial and gender diversity. More recent versions of *Disciple* have included studies of particular books of the Bible in greater depth (*Disciple II*, for example, covers Genesis, Exodus, Luke, and Acts). See www.cokesbury.com.

The United Methodist Bishops' Initiative on Children and Poverty

In 1996, the bishops of The United Methodist Church authorized an initiative in response to the economic, spiritual, emotional, and political crises facing the world's children. The goals of the initiative were to reshape The United Methodist Church in response to the God who is present among "the least of these" (Matthew 25), to help congregations understand the plight of children and respond in concrete ways, and to promote holistic evangelization among children.

Through the initiative, the bishops exercised the teaching office in the tradition of the church, as seen in the "Biblical and Theological Foundation Document." The initiative also includes a process for congregations to evaluate their own mission to children, and a link to the General Board of Global Ministries and its work with the children of Africa. The initiative includes resources for Bible Study, worship, political action, Christian education, and evangelism. For more information see www.umc.org/initiative/.

The United Methodist Hymnal

The preface to the 1989 *Hymnal* begins with these words: "From the time of John and Charles Wesley, Methodist and Evangelical United Brethren hymnals have constituted the 'worship book' of our corporate and private piety and praise. . . . From our beginning we have been 'a singing people'" (p. v). The *Hymnal* includes over six hundred hymns, ranging from traditional to contemporary, gospel to spiritual, medieval to recent. The hymns are arranged in a theologically ordered manner: the glory of God, the grace of Jesus Christ, the power of the Holy Spirit; the prevenient, justifying and sanctifying grace of God in human life; the church's response through mission, sacrament, ritual and life; and the movement toward a new heaven and a new earth (consummation).

The *Hymnal* also includes a full Psalter, in recognition of the centrality of the Psalms in the worship of the church (and Israel) across the ages, and services of baptism, Holy Communion, marriage, and death and resurrection are included. Creeds (ancient and more recent) are included, as are services of morning and evening prayer.

Although the *Hymnal* is essential for corporate worship in The United Methodist Church, many have also discovered its value as a resource for personal devotion. More recent supplements include *Songs of Zion* (African American tradition) and *The Faith We Sing.*

The United Methodist Book of Worship

Along with the *Hymnal, The Book of Worship* serves as the primary text for the planning and implementation of United Methodist worship. *The Book of Worship* assumes a balance of Word and Table in corporate worship, and offers eucharistic prayers for each season of the church year. Also included are services for baptism, marriage, and death and resurrection.

There is within this basic framework, however, a diversity of spiritual resources reflecting the multicultural character of the Church; included is a service of Las Posadas, a service of shelter for the Holy Family out of the Hispanic tradition, suggested hymns and a reading for the commemoration of Martin Luther King, Jr.'s birthday, and Christian prayers in the Korean and Native American traditions. *The Book of Worship* also responds to life situations that call forth new ways of worshiping together: ministry with persons with AIDS, a service of hope after the loss of pregnancy, a service for the blessing of animals, and a midweek service of prayer and testimony.

The Book of Worship is a wonderful resource for the practice of Christian worship, both individual and corporate. It reflects many of the strengths of United Methodist tradition: it is scriptural, it relies upon the wider Christian tradition, and yet it connects with the experiences of men and women of faith.

The Walk to Emmaus

The year 2003 marked the twenty-fifth anniversary of this spiritual retreat launched by the Upper Room. The "Walk to Emmaus," which takes its name from the experience recorded in Luke 24:13-35, is designed to develop Christian leaders through a weekend of spiritual renewal. The retreat typically gathers together 30 to 40 women or men in one place, and a team of laity and clergy serves them. In the weekend participants will listen to talks (most of them by laity), receive Holy Communion, meditate on Scripture, engage in silence, and experience small group fellowship. As a followup, many Emmaus participants participate in reunion groups that provide accountability and focus on the spiritual practices of piety, study, and action.

Approximately 40,000 persons attend "Walk to Emmaus" each year, and over half a million "pilgrims" have participated in the "Walk" since 1978. The retreat is thoroughly evangelical and catholic, in the best sense of both of these words. The Upper Room, a division of the General Board of Discipleship of The United Methodist Church, oversees the "Walk to Emmaus," which has now spread to over 70 international communities. See www.upperroom.org.

Methodist Federation for Social Action

Founded in 1908 by several Methodist Episcopal Church pastors (including Frank Mason North, who composed the hymn "Where Cross the Crowded Ways of Life"), the Methodist Federation for Social Action (MFSA) is, according to its Web site, an "independent organization uniting United Methodist activists to take action Justice, Peace and Liberation issues in the world." The MFSA's focus is on the transformation of the social order, a mission that was derived from its origins in the Social Gospel movement. The organization comprises thirty-seven chapters and a national headquarters based in Washington, D.C.

The work of the Methodist Federation for Social Action includes action and advocacy, a prayer network, a theological affirmation, and current information of particular issues. As a movement identified with the Methodist tradition, MFSA addresses the church's need to engage in "acts of justice" (see Covenant Discipleship), and within the wider biblical witness magnifies the voices of the prophets on behalf of the powerless. See also "The World Methodist Social Affirmation" in The United Methodist Hymnal (Nashville: United Methodist Publishing House, 1989), p. 886, and www.mfsaweb.org.

The Academy of Spiritual Formation

The Academy of Spiritual Formation is a two-year, intensive exposure to an environment of academic learning and spiritual disciplines. The Academy meets in different regions of the United States for five days each quarter, and is open to laity and clergy. The Academy includes morning and evening prayer each day, Holy Communion, times of silence, covenant group meetings, teaching sessions, and spiritual reading. The courses include Old and New Testaments, Christian tradition (broadly ecumenical), and practical issues related to Christian spirituality.

The Academy of Spiritual Formation is designed for individuals who take the spiritual life and growth in grace very seriously. While it includes many of the practices that are inherent in Methodism (searching the Scriptures, Holy Communion, singing, testimony, conferencing), it is ecumenical in orientation. See www.upperroom.org/academy/default.asp.

Covenant Discipleship

Covenant Discipleship is a small group ministry within the tradition of Wesleyan practice. As a movement within the church, it focuses on the rediscovery of this context for mutual accountability as a means of growth in God's grace and Christian discipleship. Covenant Discipleship groups meet for one hour a week, and write a covenant with each other. Their purpose, "to watch over one another in love," is achieved by attention to a balance of compassion, justice, worship, and devotion.

Covenant Discipleship groups have developed in response to the historical investigation and writings of David Lowes Watson. Resources for these groups are available through the General Board of Discipleship of The United Methodist Church. Meetings can also include Holy Communion, and commitments to the groups can be made in the Service of Covenant Renewal (see *The United Methodist Book of Worship* (Nashville, United Methodist Publishing House, 1992) p. 288). For more information see www.gbod.org/smallgroup/accountable/covenant.html.

Volunteers in Mission

Volunteers in Mission has been a grassroots movement in response to the desire of many laity across the church to share their gifts in "hands-on" mission. The origins of the movement came from geographical jurisdictions, General Board of Global Ministries (at the denominational level), and by countless congregations (in local communities). The mission statement of United Methodist Volunteers in Mission is reflective of the movement's aims: "UMVIM creates mission opportunities through which followers of Jesus Christ share their gifts in ministry by: serving in partnership, learning experientially, building relationships, and sharing the faith experience. Our theme is: Christian love in action!"

Volunteers in mission have responded to human needs in the following contexts: churches burned by arson, children with AIDS, and areas devastated by floods and earthquakes. They have also partnered with autonomous Methodist churches in helping to construct church facilities and schools. For more information see www.gbgm-umc.org and www.umvim.org. See also the work of the United Methodist Committee on Relief (UMCOR). These mission organizations fulfill the traditional Wesleyan emphasis on works of mercy and compassion.

The Order of Saint Luke

The Order of Saint Luke (OSL) was founded in 1946, and is an Affiliate Organization of the Section on Worship of the General Board of Discipleship. The Order of Saint Luke promotes sacramental and liturgical scholarship, education, and practice within

The United Methodist Church. The OSL is a religious order that includes laity and clergy, men and women, who are dispersed in the world and yet united in the common purpose of the order, to recover the importance of John and Charles Wesley in bringing about sacramental and evangelical revival in the Church of England. This occurs through the Order's publications and in the personal and corporate practices of members. The OSL also has a Rule of Life and Service which includes praying the daily office. See also the "Orders of Daily Praise and Prayer" in *The United Methodist Hymnal*, pp. 876-79, and www.saint-luke.org.

The Lay Speaking Ministry

United Methodist Lay Speakers are members of local congregations who are willing to serve through the gift of exhortation (see Romans 12:8). They receive training in Scripture, tradition, and the art of communication. Lay Speakers are recognized by their local churches and certified by districts of The United Methodist Church.

Although Lay Speakers are commonly seen as individuals who supply pulpits when the clergy are away, their connection with Methodism can be traced to the time of John Wesley. Known as "exhorters," they would speak in communities in the absence of preachers (indeed this was the practice of Susanna Wesley). John Wesley developed a method for lay speakers to be recommended for this task, and the tradition continued in American Methodism. Lay Speakers embody the practice of testimony, and can be particularly effective in relating their Christian experience to life in the world. See *The Book of Discipline* (Nashville: United Methodist Publishing House, 2000), ¶ 266, and www.layspeaking.org.

Upper Room Daily Devotional

The Upper Room Daily Devotional is a resource that supports the longing of many to have a regular time each day in prayer and devotion. The Home Missions Board of the Methodist Episcopal Church, South began the magazine in 1935 in response to a request from a Sunday school class in a local church in Texas.

Today *The Upper Room* is published in 44 languages and circulated in over 100 countries. See www.upperroom.org.

Practicing Our Faith

This is an ecumenical text that is ideal for study in small groups (a guide is available). Thirteen contributors explore twelve Christian practices: honoring the body, hospitality, household economics, saying yes and saying no, keeping sabbath, testimony, discernment, shaping communities, forgiveness, healing, dying well, and singing our lives. Some of the chapters seem directly relevant to the purpose of this book—singing and testimony, for example; others, such as forgiveness and discernment, have a substantial relationship but could not be pursued here. The chapter on hospitality includes a moving description of a service of Las Posadas in light of the human experience of abuse and the search for sanctuary. If you want to explore the concept of practices in a further way, *Practicing Our Faith*, ed. Dorothy C. Bass (San Francisco: Jossey-Bass, 1997) is the place to begin.

Appendix Two:
The Nature, Design, and General Rules of Our United Societies

The Nature, Design, and General Rules of Our United Societies

In the latter end of the year 1739 eight or ten persons came to Mr. Wesley, in London, who appeared to be deeply convinced of sin, and earnestly groaning for redemption. They desired, as did two or three more the next day, that he would spend some time with them in prayer, and advise them how to flee from the wrath to come, which they saw continually hanging over their heads. That he might have more time for this great work, he appointed a day when they might all come together, which from thenceforward they did every week, namely, on Thursday in the evening. To these, and as many more as desired to join with them (for their number increased daily), he gave those advices from time to time which he judged most needful for them, and they always concluded their meeting with prayer suited to their several necessities.

This was the rise of the **United Society,** first in Europe, and then in America. Such a society is no other than "a company of men having the *form* and seeking the *power* of godliness, united in order to pray together, to receive the word of exhortation, and to watch over one another in love, that they may help each other to work out their salvation."

That it may the more easily be discerned whether they are indeed working out their own salvation, each society is divided into smaller companies, called **classes,** according to their respective places of abode. There are about twelve persons in a class, one of whom is styled the **leader.** It is his duty:

1. To see each person in his class once a week at least, in order: (1) to inquire how their souls prosper; (2) to advise, reprove, comfort or exhort, as occasion may require; (3) to receive what they are willing to give toward the relief of the preachers, church, and poor.

2. To meet the ministers and the stewards of the society once a week, in order: (1) to inform the minister of any that are sick, or of any that walk disorderly and will not be reproved; (2) to pay the stewards what they have received of their several classes in the week preceding.

There is only one condition previously required of those who desire admission into these societies: "a desire to flee from the wrath to come, and to be saved from their sins." But wherever this is really fixed in the soul it will be shown by its fruits.

It is therefore expected of all who continue therein that they should continue to evidence their desire of salvation,

First: By doing no harm, by avoiding evil of every kind, especially that which is most generally practiced, such as:

The taking of the name of God in vain.

The profaning the day of the Lord, either by doing ordinary work therein or by buying or selling.

Drunkenness: buying or selling spirituous liquors, or drinking them, unless in case of extreme necessity.

Slaveholding; buying or selling slaves.

Fighting, quarreling, brawling, brother going to law with brother; returning evil for evil, or railing for railing; the using many words in buying or selling.

The buying or selling goods that have not paid the duty.

The giving or taking things on usury—i.e., unlawful interest.

Uncharitable or unprofitable conversation; particularly speaking evil of magistrates or of ministers.

Doing to others as we would not they should do unto us.

Doing what we know is not for the glory of God, as:

The putting on of gold and costly apparel.

The taking such diversions as cannot be used in the name of the Lord Jesus.

The singing those songs, or reading those books, which do not tend to the knowledge or love of God.

Softness and needless self-indulgence.

Laying up treasure upon earth.

Borrowing without a probability of paying; or taking up goods without a probability of paying for them.

It is expected of all who continue in these societies that they should continue to evidence their desire of salvation.

Secondly: By doing good; by being in every kind merciful after their power; as they have opportunity, doing good of every possible sort, and, as far as possible, to all men:

To their bodies, of the ability which God giveth, by giving food to the hungry, by clothing the naked, by visiting or helping them that are sick or in prison.

To their souls, by instructing, reproving, or exhorting all we have any intercourse with; trampling under foot that enthusiastic doctrine that "we are not to do good unless *our hearts be free to it.*"

By doing good, especially to them that are of the household of faith or groaning so to be; employing them preferably to others; buying one of another, helping each other in business, and so much the more because the world will love its own and them only.

By all possible diligence and frugality, that the gospel be not blamed.

By running with patience the race which is set before them, denying themselves, and taking up their cross daily; submitting to bear the reproach of Christ, to be as the filth and offscouring of the world; and looking that men should say all manner of evil of them *falsely,* for the Lord's sake.

It is expected of all who desire to continue in these societies that they should continue to evidence their desire of salvation,

Thirdly: By attending upon all the ordinances of God; such are:

The public worship of God.

The ministry of the Word, either read or expounded.

The Supper of the Lord.

Family and private prayer.

Searching the Scriptures.

Fasting or abstinence.

These are the General Rules of our societies; all of which we are taught of God to observe, even in his written Word, which is the only rule, and the sufficient rule, both of our faith and practice. And all these we know his Spirit writes on truly awakened hearts. If there be any among us who observe them not, who habitually break any of them, let it be known unto them who watch over that soul as they who must give an account. We will admonish him of the error of his ways. We will bear with him for a season. But then, if he repent not, he hath no more place among us. We have delivered our own souls.

Appendix Three:
A Service of Covenant Renewal

COVENANT RENEWAL SERVICE

In 1663 Richard Alleine, a Puritan, published Vindiciae Pietatis: or, A Vindication of Godliness in the Greater Strictness and Spirituality of It. *In 1753, it was again published in John Wesley's* A Christian Library. *Wesley used one chapter, "The Application of the Whole," on Monday, August 11, 1755, in what probably was the first real celebration of the Covenant Service in the Methodist movement.*

Wesley found the service rich and meaningful, as expressed in his Journal: "Many mourned before God, and many were comforted" (April 1756); "It was, as usual, a time of remarkable blessing" (October 1765); "It was an occasion for a variety of spiritual experiences . . . I do not know that ever we had a greater blessing. Afterwards many desired to return thanks, either for a sense of pardon, for full salvation, or for a fresh manifestation of His graces, healing all their backslidings" (January 1, 1775). In London these services were usually held on New Year's Day. Around the country the Covenant Service was conducted whenever John Wesley visited the Methodist Societies.

After the time of Wesley several versions of the Covenant Service were developed, gradually giving Wesley's material less place in the total service. The present service follows our Basic Pattern of worship, enables the congregation to participate more fully, and updates language. Most significant, the liturgy beginning with the Invitation is taken directly from Wesley's service of 1780.

The heart of the service, focused in the Covenant Prayer, requires persons to commit themselves to God. This covenant is serious and assumes adequate preparation for and continual response to the covenant. Leaders of worship must take seriously the need to prepare the congregation for this service, possibly through study sessions and prayer. The leaders must also assume responsibility to assist persons to be faithful to the covenant, possibly through meetings for spiritual discipline.

The Covenant Service is most commonly held on New Year's Eve or Day and therefore is sometimes called a Watch Night Service. Historically, a Watch Night Service would be three hours or longer, including readings from Scripture and hymn singing. This Covenant Service would also be appropriate on one of the Sundays After the Epiphany, during Lent, on a church anniversary, or during a revival or preaching mission. Ideally, the service should be used only once a year on the same Sunday. Red is an appropriate color for paraments and vestments.

Individual copies of the Covenant Service are recommended for all worshipers so that they may sign and keep them as reminders.

ENTRANCE

GATHERING *See 16-17.* [Page numbers in this appendix refer to pages in *The United Methodist Book of Worship.*]

GREETING * ["An asterisk (*) indicates an act of worship for which the congregation may be invited to stand" (*United Methodist Book of Worship*, p. 12).] *See 17-20.*

HYMN * **Come, Let Us Use the Grace Divine (*UMH* 606)**

Charles Wesley wrote this hymn specifically for this service.

OPENING PRAYER * *See 20-21.*

O God, Searcher of all our hearts,
   you have formed us as a people and claimed us for your
   own.

As we come to acknowledge your sovereignty and grace,
and to enter anew into covenant with you,
reveal any reluctance or falsehood within us.
Let your Spirit impress your truth on our inmost being,
and receive us in mercy, for the sake of our Mediator,
Jesus Christ,
who lives and reigns with you in the unity of the Holy Spirit,
one God, for ever and ever. Amen.

(DAVID TRIPP, ENGLAND, 20TH CENT.)

LITANY OF THANKSGIVING

The following or another litany of thanksgiving may be used:

Let us give thanks for all of God's mercies.

O God, our Covenant Friend,
you have been gracious to us through all the years of our
lives.
We thank you for your loving care,
which has filled our days and brought us to this time and
place.
We praise your holy name, O God.

You have given us life and reason,
and set us in a world filled with your glory.
You have comforted us with family and friends,
and ministered to us through the hands of our sisters
and brothers. **R** ["**R** indicates that the congregation repeat
their response" (*United Methodist Book of Worship*, p. 12).]

You have filled our hearts with a hunger after you,
and have given us your peace.
You have redeemed us, and called us to a high calling in
Christ Jesus.
You have given us a place in the fellowship of your Spirit
and the witness of your Church. **R**

You have been our light in darkness
and a rock of strength in adversity and temptation.
You have been the very Spirit of joy in our joys
and the all-sufficient reward in all our labors. **R**

You remembered us when we forgot you.
You followed us even when we tried to flee from you.
You met us with forgiveness when we returned to you.
For all your patience and overflowing grace. **R**

PROCLAMATION

PRAYER FOR ILLUMINATION * *See 22.*

SCRIPTURE LESSON(S)

These lessons may be interspersed with hymns (see 294) and psalms:

Deuteronomy 31:9-13	A covenant renewal
2 Kings 23:1-3	Renewal of covenant
2 Chronicles 34:29-33	Renewal of covenant
Jeremiah 31:31-34	A new covenant
Psalm 50 (UMH 783)	Gathering of the faithful
1 Peter 1	Call of holy living
Matthew 25:14-30	Parable of talents
Matthew 25:31-46	Judgment of the nations
John 15:1-8	Jesus is the true vine.

PROCLAMATION

Brothers and sisters in Christ,
the Christian life is redeemed from sin and consecrated to God.
Through baptism, we have entered this life
and have been admitted into the new covenant
of which Jesus Christ is the Mediator.
He sealed it with his own blood, that it might last for ever.

On the one side, God promises to give us new life in Christ,
the Source and Perfecter of our faith.
On the other side, we are pledged
to live no more for ourselves but only for Jesus Christ,
who loved us and gave himself for us.

From time to time we renew our covenant with God,
especially when we reaffirm the Baptismal Covenant
and gather at the Lord's table.

Today, however, we meet, as the generations before us have met,
to renew the covenant that binds us to God.
Let us make this covenant of God our own.

WESLEY'S COVENANT SERVICE

INVITATION

Commit yourselves to Christ as his servants.
Give yourselves to him, that you may belong to him.
Christ has many services to be done.
Some are more easy and honorable,
    others are more difficult and disgraceful.
Some are suitable to our inclinations and interests,
    others are contrary to both.
In some we may please Christ and please ourselves.
But then there are other works where we cannot please Christ
    except by denying ourselves.
It is necessary, therefore,
    that we consider what it means to be a servant of Christ.

Let us, therefore, go to Christ, and pray:

Let me be your servant, under your command.
I will no longer be my own.
I will give up myself to your will in all things.

Be satisfied that Christ shall give you your place and work.

Lord, make me what you will.
I put myself fully into your hands:
    put me to doing, put me to suffering,
    let me be employed for you, or laid aside for you,
    let me be full, let me be empty,
    let me have all things, let me have nothing.
I freely and with a willing heart
    give it all to your pleasure and disposal.

Christ will be the Savior of none but his servants.
He is the source of all salvation to those who obey.

Christ will have no servants except by consent;
Christ will not accept anything except full consent
    to all that he requires.
Christ will be all in all, or he will be nothing.

Confirm this by a holy covenant.

To make this covenant a reality in your life, listen to these
    admonitions:

First, set apart some time, more than once,
    to be spent alone before the Lord;
in seeking earnestly God's special assistance
    and gracious acceptance of you;
in carefully thinking through all the conditions of the covenant;
in searching your hearts
    whether you have already freely given your life to Christ.
Consider what your sins are.
Consider the laws of Christ, how holy, strict, and spiritual they
    are, and whether you, after having carefully considered them,
    are willing to choose them all.
Be sure you are clear in these matters, see that you do not
    lie to God.

Second, be serious and in a spirit of holy awe and reverence.

Third, claim God's covenant,
rely upon God's promise of giving grace and strength,
    so you can keep your promise.
Trust not your own strength and power.

Fourth, resolve to be faithful.
You have given to the Lord your hearts,
    you have opened your mouths to the Lord,
    and you have dedicated yourself to God.
With God's power, never go back.

And last, be then prepared to renew your covenant with
    the Lord.
Fall down on your knees, lift your hands toward heaven,
    open your hearts to the Lord, as we pray:

COVENANT PRAYER

The people kneel or bow.

O righteous God, for the sake of your Son Jesus Christ,
   see me as I fall down before you.
Forgive my unfaithfulness in not having done your will,
   for you have promised mercy to me
   if I turn to you with my whole heart.

God requires that you shall put away all your idols.

I here from the bottom of my heart renounce them all,
   covenanting with you that no known sin shall be
   allowed in my life.
Against your will, I have turned my love toward the world.
In your power,
   I will watch all temptations that will lead me away
   from you.
For my own righteousnes is riddled with sin,
   unable to stand before you.

Through Christ, God has offered to be your God again
   if you would let him.

Before all heaven and earth,
   I here acknowledge you as my Lord and God.
I take you, Father, Son, and Holy Spirit, for my portion,
   and vow to give up myself, body and soul, as your servant,
   to serve you in holiness and righteousness all the days
   of my life.

God has given the Lord Jesus Christ
   as the only way and means of coming to God.

Jesus, I do here on bended knees accept Christ
   as the only new and living Way,
   and sincerely join myself in a covenant with him.
O blessed Jesus, I come to you,
   hungry, sinful, miserable, blind, and naked,
   unworthy even to wash the feet of your servants.
I do here, with all my power, accept you as my Lord and Head.
I renounce my own worthiness,

and vow that you are the Lord, my righteousness.
I renounce my own wisdom, and take you for my own guide.
I renounce my own will, and take your will as my law.

Christ has told you that you must suffer with him.

I do here covenant with you, O Christ,
  to take my lot with you as it may fall.
Through your grace I promise
  that neither life nor death shall part me from you.

God has given holy laws as the rule of your life.

I do here willingly put my neck under your yoke, to carry
  your burden.
All your laws are holy, just, and good.
I therefore take them as the rule for my words, thoughts,
  and actions,
promising that I will strive
    to order my whole life according to your direction,
    and not allow myself to neglect anything I know to be my
    duty.

The almighty God searches and knows your heart.

O God, you know that I make this covenant with you
  today without guile or reservation.
If any falsehood should be in it, guide me and help me
  to set it aright.
And now, glory be to you, O God the Father,
  whom I from this day forward shall look upon as my God
  and Father.
Glory be to you, O God the Son,
  who have loved me and washed me from my sins in your
  own blood, and now is my Savior and Redeemer.
Glory be to you, O God the Holy Spirit,
  who by your almighty power have turned my heart
  from sin to God.

O mighty God, the Lord Omnipotent, Father, Son, and Holy
  Spirit, you have now become my Covenant Friend.
And I, through your infinite grace, have become your
  covenant servant.

So be it.
And let the covenant I have made on earth be ratified in
heaven.
Amen.

You are advised to make this covenant not only in your heart, but in word; not only in word, but in writing. Therefore, with all reverence, lay the service before the Lord as your act and deed. And when you have done this, sign it. Then keep it as a reminder of the holy agreement between God and you that you may remember it during doubts and temptations.

See also A Covenant Prayer in the Wesleyan Tradition (UMH 607).

The pastor may now celebrate Holy Communion, the people using A Service of Word and Table III (UMH 15) or one of the musical settings (UMH 17-25) and the pastor using The Great Thanksgiving on 58-59. Otherwise, the service continues as follows:

HYMN * *Suggested from* UMH:

563/4 Father, We Thank you   117 O God, Our Help in Ages Past
698 God of The Ages   501 O Thou Who Camest from
561 Jesus, United by Thy Grace   Above

DISMISSAL WITH BLESSING * *See 31-32.*

Notes

Introduction: Spiritual Practices for United Methodists

1. Randy L. Maddox, *Responsible Grace* (Nashville: Kingswood, 1994), p. 69.

2. See Dorothy C. Bass, "Keeping Sabbath," *Practicing Our Faith*, ed. Dorothy C. Bass (San Francisco: Jossey-Bass, 1997) and Dorothy C. Bass, *Receiving the Day: Christian Practices for Opening the Gift of Time* (San Francisco: Jossey-Bass, 2000).

3. L. Gregory Jones, "Faith Matters: Apprenticeship," *Christian Century* 114, no. 21 (1997): 669. Copyright 1997 *Christian Century*. Reprinted with permission from the July 16-23, 1997, issue of the *Christian Century*.

4. Stanley Hauerwas, *After Christendom?* (Nashville: Abingdon Press, 1991), pp. 101-3.

5. Ibid., p. 103.

6. *The United Methodist Hymnal* (Nashville: United Methodist Publishing House, 1989), p. 40.

7. See the excellent essay by M. Shawn Copeland, "Saying Yes and Saying No," in *Practicing Our Faith*, ed. Dorothy C. Bass (San Francisco: Jossey-Bass, 1997).

8. Alasdair C. MacIntyre, *After Virtue* (Notre Dame, Ind.: University of Notre Dame Press, 1981), p. 207.

9. Peter Storey, *With God in the Crucible* (Nashville: Abingdon Press, 2002).

10. Malcolm Warford, *Becoming a New Church* (Cleveland: United Church Press, 2000), p. 29.

11. Miroslav Volf argues that "people come to believe either because they find themselves already engaged in Christian practices (say, by being raised in a Christian home) or because they are attracted to them. In most cases, Christian practices come first and Christian beliefs follow" in "Theology for a Way of Life," *Practicing Theology*, ed. Miroslav Volf and Dorothy C. Bass (Grand Rapids: Eerdmans, 2002), p. 256.

12. See Eugene H. Peterson, *A Long Obedience in the Same Direction* (Downers Grove, Ill.: InterVarsity Press, 2000).

13. Craig Dykstra, *Growing in the Life of Faith* (Louisville, Ky.: Geneva Press, 1999), p. 11.

14. This is the profound insight of Albert C. Outler. See *John Wesley*, ed. Albert C. Outler (New York: Oxford University Press, 1964), pp. 9-10.

15. Dorothy C. Bass and Craig Dykstra, "Growing in the Practices of Faith," in *Practicing Our Faith*, ed. Dorothy C. Bass (San Francisco: Jossey-Bass, 1997), p. 203.

16. "Weave, Weave" by Rosemary Crow is found in Elise S. Eslinger, ed. *The Upper Room Worshipbook: Music and Liturgies for Spiritual Formation* (Nashville: Upper Room, 1985), p. 48.

17. *The United Methodist Book of Worship* (Nashville: United Methodist Publishing House, 1992), p. 88.

18. I am aware of the discussion, and the advice often given at gatherings of church leaders and pastors about downplaying or hiding the denominational identity. The rationale of this book is that such a move has disastrous unintended consequences: we divorce ourselves from the riches of our faith tradition, and we are more prone to adopt the prevailing norms of the culture, whether these be consumer-driven, psychotherapeutic, or political.

19. Rueben P. Job, *A Wesleyan Spiritual Reader* (Nashville: Abingdon Press, 1997), pp. 194-95.

20. *The United Methodist Book of Worship*, p. 291. For a wonderful commentary on the covenant prayer, see Keith Beasley-Topliffe, *Surrendering to God* (Brewster, Mass.: Paraclete Press, 2001).

21. *The United Methodist Hymnal*, p. 607.

1. Searching the Scriptures

1. 2 Timothy 3:17. Wesley's discussion of "searching the Scriptures" in this sermon is largely based on 2 Timothy 3:15-17.

2. See "The Means of Grace," *The Bicentennial Edition of the Works of John Wesley*, vol. 1, (Nashville: Abingdon, 1984), p. 387.

3. *A Wesleyan Spiritual Reader* (Nashville: Abingdon Press, 1997), p. 85.

4. John Wesley, preface to *Explanatory Notes on the New Testament* (New York: Methodist Episcopal Church, 1818), p. v.

5. See "The Way to the Kingdom," based on Mark 1:15, in *John Wesley's Forty-four Sermons* (London: Epworth Press, 1944), pp. 79-84.

6. Albert C. Outler, *Evangelism and Theology in the Wesleyan Spirit* (Nashville: Discipleship Resources, 1996), p. 110.

7. Ibid., p. 130.

8. A version of this appears in *Upper Room Disciplines*, 2003 (Nashville: The Upper Room, 2002).

9. See Dick Murray, *Teaching the Bible to Adults and Youth* (Nashville: Abingdon Press, 1987) and "Praying the Bible," *Weavings* XI, no. 4 (1996). This is also what Rueben P. Job describes as "spiritual reading" in *A Wesleyan Spiritual Reader*.

10. See appendix 1.

2. Generosity with the Poor

1. Kenneth L. Carder, "Proclaiming the Gospel of Grace," in *Theology and Evangelism in the Wesleyan Heritage*, ed. James C. Logan (Nashville: Kingswood, 1994), p. 87.

2. See *The Works of John Wesley*, vol. 8 (London: Zondervan, 1872), pp. 269-71. These became the General Rules of the Methodist Church, as found in *The Book of Discipline of The United Methodist Church* (Nashville: United Methodist Publishing House, 2000), ¶ 103.

3. David Lowes Watson, *Covenant Discipleship* (Nashville: Discipleship Resources, 1991), p. 84.

4. Kenneth L. Carder, "Proclaiming the Gospel of Grace," in *Theology and Evangelism in the Wesleyan Heritage*, pp. 84-85.

5. Theodore W. Jennings Jr., "Good News to the Poor in the Wesleyan Heritage," in *Theology and Evangelism in the Wesleyan Heritage*, pp. 140-56. For an excellent summary of Wesley's personal practices in relation to money and the poor, see Kenneth L. Carder, "Wesley and Giving" (paper presented at The Giving and the Gospel Symposium, Nashville, Tenn., October 23, 1997). "One cannot adequately understand or appropriate Wesley apart from his convictions and practices regarding money and its use," Carder insists in this lecture.

6. *The Works of John Wesley*, vol. 13 (London: Zondervan, 1872), p. 258.

7. Ibid., p. 260.

8. Kenneth L. Carder, "Proclaiming the Gospel of Grace," in *Theology and Evangelism in the Wesleyan Heritage*, p. 85.

9. John Wesley, "Upon Our Lord's Sermon on the Mount," Sermon XXIII, *John Wesley's Forty-four Sermons* (London: Epworth Press, 1944), pp. 305-22.

10. See Sondra Ely Wheeler, *Wealth as Peril and Obligation* (Grand Rapids: Eerdmans, 1995), pp. 123-34.

11. See Craig Dykstra's discussion in *Growing in the Life of Faith* (Louisville, Ky.: Geneva Press, 1999), pp. 90-91.

12. See "The Economic Community," *The Book of Discipline of The United Methodist Church* (Nashville: United Methodist Publishing House, 2000), ¶ 163.

13. Perry C. Ainsworth, "The Kingdom for the Poor," *Weavings* 15, no. 1 (2000): 31.

14. Paraphrased from John Wesley's "Thoughts on Methodism," from a lecture by Bishop Kenneth Carder. See Wesley's sermons, "On God's Vineyard" and "On the Use of Money." The sketch of Wesley's life is also taken from that lecture, presented at "Giving and the Gospel: A Symposium Sponsored by the General Board of Discipleship," October 24, 1997.

3. Testimony

1. One of the strengths of the African American church is the blending together of singing and testimony. Note the hymn "Stand by Me" (*The United Methodist Hymnal*, 512), composed by Charles Albert Tindley, the self-educated son of slaves who preached to a Methodist Church of over twelve thousand members. For a commentary see Paul W. Chilcote, "A Faith That Sings," *The Wesleyan Tradition: A Paradigm for Renewal* (Nashville: Abingdon Press, 2002), p. 155.

2. Thomas Hoyt Jr., "Testimony," in *Practicing Our Faith*, ed. Dorothy C. Bass (San Francisco: Jossey-Bass, 1997), p. 92.

3. Note the hymn "Where Shall My Wandering Soul Begin," considered to be Charles Wesley's reflection on his own conversion, in *The United Methodist Hymnal* (Nashville: The United Methodist Publishing House, 1989), p. 342.

4. *John Wesley*, ed. Albert C. Outler (Oxford: Oxford University Press, 1964), p. 51. For the experience of the apostle Paul on the road to Damascus, see Acts 9.

5. *The Bicentennial Edition of the Works of John Wesley*, vol. 18 (Nashville: Abingdon Press, 1988), pp. 249-50.

6. Roberta C. Bondi, "Aldersgate and Patterns of Methodist Spirituality," in *Aldersgate Reconsidered*, ed. Randy L. Maddox (Nashville: Kingswood, 1990), pp. 21-22.

7. Ibid., p. 25.

8. *John Wesley*, p. 51. Note the Journals of John Wesley from September 1738 to April 1739.

9. David Lowes Watson, "Aldersgate Street and The General Rules: The Form and the Power of Methodist Discipleship," in *Aldersgate Reconsidered*, pp. 44-45.

10. Craig Dykstra, *Growing in the Life of Faith* (Louisville, Ky.: Geneva Press, 1999), p. 41.

11. Martin Luther, *Works,* vol. XVIII, ed. Jaroslav Pelikan (St. Louis: Concordia, 1955), p. 191.

12. Anthony B. Robinson, *Good News in Exile* (Grand Rapids: Eerdmans, 1999), p. 23.

13. See the essay by Serene Jones, "Graced Practices: Excellence and Freedom in the Christian Life," in *Practicing Theology,* ed. Miroslav Volf and Dorothy C. Bass (Grand Rapids: Eerdmans, 2002).

14. Ibid., p. 66.

4. Singing

1. Note the excellent essay by United Methodist theologian and musician Don E. Saliers, "Singing Our Lives," in *Practicing Our Faith,* ed. Dorothy C. Bass (San Francisco: Jossey-Bass, 1997).

2. Geoffrey Wainwright, *Doxology: The Praise of God in Worship, Doctrine, and Life* (New York: Oxford University Press, 1980), p. 201. Wainwright provides an excellent discussion of the relationship between poetry and piety.

3. "Hark! the Herald Angels Sing," *The United Methodist Hymnal* (Nashville: The United Methodist Publishing House, 1989), p. 240.

4. "Christ, Whose Glory Fills the Skies," *The United Methodist Hymnal,* p. 173.

5. Ibid.

6. "And Can It Be that I Should Gain," *The United Methodist Hymnal,* p. 363.

7. "O Love Divine, What Hast Thou Done," *The United Methodist Hymnal,* p. 287.

8. " 'Tis Finished! The Messiah Dies," *The United Methodist Hymnal,* p. 282.

9. "Christ the Lord Is Risen Today," *The United Methodist Hymnal,* p. 302.

10. "Spirit of Faith, Come Down," *The United Methodist Hymnal,* p. 332.

11. "A Charge to Keep I Have," *The United Methodist Hymnal,* p. 413.

12. "Come, Thou Long-Expected Jesus," *The United Methodist Hymnal,* p. 196. For a commentary that places this hymn in the historical context of Charles Wesley's response to the evil of human slavery in the eighteenth century see S T Kimbrough Jr., *Lost in Wonder* (Nashville: Upper Room, 1987), p. 52.

13. *Practicing Our Faith,* ed. Dorothy C. Bass (San Francisco: Jossey-Bass, 1997), p. 5.

14. "Directions for Singing" from John Wesley's *Select Hymns,* 1761; cited in *The United Methodist Hymnal,* p. vii.

15. Lester Ruth, "Word and Table: A Balanced Model for Wesleyan Worship," in *The Wesleyan Tradition: A Paradigm for Renewal* (Nashville: Abingdon Press, 2002), p. 146.

16. "The Church of Christ in Every Age," *The United Methodist Hymnal,* p. 589. "The Church of Christ in Every Age" by Fred Pratt Green © 1971 Hope Publishing Co., Carol Stream, IL 60188. All rights reserved. Used by permission.

17. "When the Church of Jesus," *The United Methodist Hymnal,* p. 592. Taken from "When the Church of Jesus" by Fred Pratt Green © 1969 Hope Publishing Co., Carol Stream, IL 60188. All rights reserved. Used by permission.

5. Holy Communion

1. "There is a temptation to turn to exemplary cases when talking about the relationship between religious beliefs and practices. . . . But there is also something to

be said for looking at efforts by less exemplary believers to bridge the troublesome gaps that keep reappearing in various ways between their beliefs and practices. Their struggles reveal the continual slippage and compromise that occur between these two central aspects of the religious life. . . . In their palpable imperfections, less exemplary believers point us away from notions of heroism and mastery in religious practice; they draw our gaze instead toward the gracious God who works in and through them." See Amy Plantinga Pauw, "Attending to the Gaps between Beliefs and Practices," in *Practicing Theology*, ed. Miroslav Volf and Dorothy C. Bass (Grand Rapids: Eerdmans, 2002), pp. 33-34.

2. "Jesus! the Name High over All," *The United Methodist Hymnal* (Nashville: The United Methodist Publishing House, 1989), p. 193.

3. "Come, Sinners, to the Gospel Feast," *The United Methodist Hymnal*, p. 616. See Luke 14:16-24.

4. "Great Is Thy Faithfulness," *The United Methodist Hymnal*, p. 140. See Exodus 16. "Great Is Thy Faithfulness" by Thomas O. Chisholm © 1923. Renewal 1951 Hope Publishing Co., Carol Stream, IL 60188. All rights reserved. Used by permission.

5. *The United Methodist Book of Worship* (Nashville: The United Methodist Publishing House, 1992), p. 58.

6. Mortimer Arias, *Announcing the Reign of God* (Philadelphia: Fortress Press, 1984), p. 81.

7. *The United Methodist Hymnal* (Nashville: United Methodist Publishing House, 1989), p. 14.

8. "Come, Let Us Join Our Friends Above," *The United Methodist Hymnal*, p. 709.

9. "Blessed Assurance," *The United Methodist Hymnal*, p. 369.

10. "Come, Sinners, to the Gospel Feast," *The United Methodist Hymnal*, p. 616.

11. For a discussion of limited and unlimited atonement, see Scott J. Jones, *United Methodist Doctrine: The Extreme Center* (Nashville: Abingdon Press, 2002), p. 181.

12. Donald H. Juel, *The Gospel of Mark* (Nashville: Abingdon Press, 1999), p. 148.

13. Although beyond the scope of this hymn, Paul thanks the Philippians for the gift from them sent by Epaphroditus: "a fragrant offering, a sacrifice acceptable and pleasing to God" (Philippians 4:18).

14. "Where there is forgiveness of these [sins], there is no longer any offering for sin" (Hebrews 10:18).

15. See Charles Wesley's "O Thou Who This Mysterious Bread," *The United Methodist Hymnal*, p. 613, based on Luke 24:13-35, the account of Jesus on the road to Emmaus.

16. See Charles Wesley's "Come, Sinners, to the Gospel Feast," *The United Methodist Hymnal*, p. 616, based on Luke 14:16-24, the invitation to the great party.

17. "The Duty of Constant Communion," *The Bicentennial Edition of the Works of John Wesley*, vol. 3 (Nashville: Abingdon Press, 1986), p. 429.

18. *The Bicentennial Edition of the Works of John Wesley*, vol. 19 (Nashville: Abingdon Press, 1990), p. 93.

19. *The United Methodist Hymnal*, p. 13.

20. Ibid., p. 14.

6. Life Together

1. Note the examination of a bishop in The United Methodist Church: "You are called to guard the faith, to seek the unity, and to exercise the discipline of the whole church." See *The United Methodist Book of Worship* (Nashville: United Methodist Publishing House, 1992), p. 703.

Notes to pages 81-92

2. Thomas A. Langford, "Doctrinal Affirmation and Theological Exploration," in *Doctrine and Theology in The United Methodist Church*, ed. Thomas A. Langford (Nashville: Kingswood, 1991), p. 204.

3. *The Book of Discipline* (Nashville: United Methodist Publishing House, 2000), ¶ 103.

4. *The Book of Discipline*, ¶ 103. See appendix 2.

5. See David Lowes Watson, *Covenant Discipleship* (Nashville: Discipleship Resources, 1991), p. 78.

6. See Dick Wills, *Waking to God's Dream* (Nashville: Abingdon Press, 1999), pp. 40-41.

7. William H. Willimon, *Acts* (Atlanta: John Knox, 1988), p. 41.

8. John Wesley, *Explanatory Notes on the New Testament* (New York: Methodist Episcopal Church, 1818), p. 548.

9. Craig Dykstra and Dorothy C. Bass, "Growing in the Practices of Faith," in *Practicing Our Faith*, ed. Dorothy C. Bass (San Francisco: Jossey-Bass, 1997), p. 202.

10. Paul Jones writes: "The essence of the Wesleyan movement was disciplined care of souls. And, characteristic of an order, every member was supposed to be under spiritual direction. . . . His passion was to promote spirituality as practice, what he called 'practical religion.' " *The Art of Spiritual Direction* (Nashville: Upper Room Books, 2002), p. 79.

11. "We Are the Church," *The United Methodist Hymnal* (Nashville: United Methodist Publishing House, 1989), p. 558.

7. A Way of Life in the World: Spiritual Practice and the Recovery of Human Nature

1. Geoffrey Wainwright, "Towards God," *Union Seminary Quarterly Review*, Supplementary Issue (1981): 13.

2. Augustine, *Confessions* (London: Penguin, 1961), I, 1, p. 21, is one of many translations.

3. Geoffrey Wainwright, *Doxology: The Praise of God in Worship, Doctrine, and Life* (New York: Oxford, 1980), p. 35.

4. Ibid., p. 37.

5. Albert C. Outler, ed. *Evangelism and Theology in the Wesleyan Spirit* (Nashville: Discipleship Resources, 1996), p. 96. See also "Predestination Calmly Considered," in *John Wesley*, ed. Albert Outler (New York: Oxford University Press, 1964).

6. See *John Wesley*, ed. Albert C. Outler (New York: Oxford University Press, 1964), p. 17.

7. See Rueben P. Job, *A Wesleyan Spiritual Reader* (Nashville: Abingdon Press, 1997), p. 112.

8. *The United Methodist Hymnal*, p. 384.

9. Thomas A. Langford, *Practical Divinity*, vol. 1 (Nashville: Abingdon Press, 1983), p. 36. Emphases added.

10. *John Wesley*, p. 153. We have not discussed fasting as a spiritual practice, although it is certainly prominent in the Scriptures and in Methodist tradition. It certainly could be discussed within the general concept of honoring the body as a form of prayer, and as a form of self-denial. In a culture that struggles with both obesity, eating disorders that lead to anorexia nervosa, and skewed messages about body images, fasting is both a relevant topic and an ambiguous one.

11. *The Bicentennial Edition of the Works of John Wesley*, vol. 1 (Nashville, Abingdon Press, 1984), p. 378.

143

12. Ibid., pp. 379-80.

13. Ibid., p. 380.

14. Ibid., p. 381.

15. Serene Jones, "Graced Practices: Excellence and Freedom in the Christian Life," in *Practicing Theology*, ed. Miroslav Volf and Dorothy C. Bass (Grand Rapids: Eerdmans, 2002), p. 65.

16. *The Bicentennial Edition of the Works of John Wesley*, vol. 1, p. 391. For a parallel reflection in the Reformed tradition, see Craig Dykstra, *Growing in the Life of Faith* (Louisville: Geneva, 1999), especially his commentary on "The Larger Catechism," p. 42.

17. Geoffrey Wainwright notes: "The proverb says that like communes with like. The first meaning of humanity's being made in the image of God is that God has made humanity sufficiently like himself for communion between God and human beings to be possible." *Doxology: The Praise of God in Worship, Doctrine, and Life*, p. 16.

18. Craig Dykstra, "Reconceiving Practice in Theological Inquiry and Education," in *Virtues and Practices in the Christian Tradition*, ed. Nancey Murphy, Brad Kallenberg, and Mark Nation (Harrisburg: Trinity Press International, 1997), p. 173.

19. *Practicing Our Faith*, ed. Dorothy C. Bass (San Francisco: Jossey-Bass, 1997), p. 5.

8. The Experience of Christ: Lives Ordered by Grace

1. Tom Long, *The Witness of Preaching* (Louisville: Westminster/John Knox, 1989), p. 16. I am also grateful to Tom Long for a conversation about doctrinal preaching.

2. "I Sought the Lord," *The United Methodist Hymnal*, p. 341.

3. Gregory S. Clapper, *As If the Heart Mattered* (Nashville: Upper Room, 1997), pp. 49-50.

4. See the sermons of John Wesley on the Sermon on the Mount, and Gregory S. Clapper's excellent discussion of "orthokardia" ("right heart") in *As If the Heart Mattered* (Nashville: Upper Room, 1997), p. 19ff.

5. *The Bicentennial Edition of the Works of John Wesley*, vol. 18 (Nashville: Abingdon Press, 1988), pp. 249-50.

6. "When in Our Music God Is Glorified," *The United Methodist Hymnal*, p. 68.

7. I heard this shared in a sermon by the Reverend Ernest Campbell, former minister of the Riverside Church in New York City.

8. "Let Us Plead for Faith Alone," *The United Methodist Hymnal*, p. 385.

9. Anne Lamott, *Bird by Bird* (New York: Anchor Books, 1994), p. 167.

10. C. S. Lewis, *The Joyful Christian* (New York: MacMillan, 1977), p. 77.

11. "Love Divine, All Loves Excelling," *The United Methodist Hymnal*, p. 384.

9. Rediscovery of Tradition as a Means of Grace

1. Martin Buber, *Tales of the Hasidim* (New York: Schocken Books, 1947), pp. 245-46.

2. Barbara Brown Taylor, *The Seeds of Heaven* (Cincinnati: Forward Movement, 1990), p. 24.

3. "O For a Thousand Tongues to Sing," *The United Methodist Hymnal*, p. 57.

4. John A. Sanford, *The Kingdom Within* (San Francisco, Harper & Row, 1987), p. 27.

5. "Hark! the Herald Angels Sing," *The United Methodist Hymnal*, p. 240.